Snapshots of American Culture:

Japanophilia and the Otaku

By M. Jean

2

Dedication

This book is dedicated to three exceptional individuals I have had the honor to meet while making my rounds in the anime con community.

For CD, whose eloquent and "edutaining" lectures ignited my curiosity about anime cons and their cultural impact in the US.

For MP, whose confidence in my first presentations gave me the final push to put pen to paper and publish these ideas.

And for JP, whose grace, professionalism, and oft-unrewarded dedication to the Anime-Con-That-Must-Not-Be-Named and its nurturing of global citizens inspire me to continue my own work for that community.

I thank you for your leadership and hope this book makes your jobs a bit easier.

Acknowledgements

Thanks first and foremost go to my Father for supporting and loving me through the trials and tribulations of my studies and intellectual pursuits.

This book would not be coherent (or as coherent as it is) if not for the tireless support of my editor Jez Springtree. I'm sure anyone who picks up this book would thank you for your effort.

This book would not be pretty (or as pretty as it is) without the aid of Meg Anderson. Her grammatical guidance in my venture into book creation has been priceless.

This book would not be published in a timely fashion (or as timely as it is) if JR Wesley did not answer my interminable questions about e-book publishing.

Thank you all.

Table of Contents

Foreword

[Lens Change: Twenty year old, Philadelphia-Based Anime Con Attendee who has attended anime cons since 2011]

The work you have before you is a collection of blog posts, lectures, and speeches from 2014. In that year, I was granted the opportunity to speak on a selection of topics about the intersections of Japanese and US American culture, as well as new media in the literary world, at a recently formed culture convention out West. It was a new experience: lectures presented at these conventions are a great departure from my public speaking education of presenting in academic settings. Edutainment is the style of choice, with the presentations feeling more like extended TED talks than academic lectures. Often quality of content is given less importance than the showmanship and performance of it. Many presenters do not even cite sources or qualify the credibility of their information. As such, the accuracy of information at any given panel or program varies greatly, and thus attendees learn organically who are the more reliable and respectable presenters.

My last talk at this particular convention was entitled "Combating Otaku Stigma, and How We Will Rule the World." (Another key difference between academic and convention settings: the need for inflammatory language, titles with exaggerated appeal, and hooks for elevator pitches to be included in the program booklet or app.) After some lively discussion of stereotypes and gender relations, the talk concluded in the maximum allotted time. Two men then approached me, giving me their business cards, and invited me to speak at another, much larger convention in California. That interaction inspired me to get serious about the topics I had presented and the many more I had contemplated during the previous months.

After returning home, recovering from a rhinovirus contracted at the convention[1], and catching up on sleep, I came to the realization that publishing these ideas would be beneficial to the community at large. By July, I had drafted an annotated outline comprised of older ideas and new, relevant material based on films, videogames, and other media that had risen in popularity. This work was polished and made into a cohesive book during the fall, and <u>Snapshots of American Culture: Japanophilia and the Otaku</u> was published shortly after the year turned to 2015.

I consider this work to be a composite of personal reflection, academic rumination, and intuitive speculation grounded in observation. It is not academic writing and has not gone through the rigors necessary to

---

[1] Contracting an illness at a con is very common as large groups of people gather in confined areas. Many con goers have horror tales of various instances of "con flu" or "con crud."

be such. I have consciously (grudgingly) allowed gaping holes, generalizations, and abundant lack of thorough research. Creating a quality academic work based in empirical study and reviewed by peers would take time, during which many of the points here would lose their significance and relevance. Therefore, academic quality has been pushed aside to allow for communication of thought, the exchange of ideas, and discussion of topics immediately pertinent.

Introduction

[Lens Change: Trilingual, international relations scholar with an academic background in politics, cultures, and the fluid exchanges and influences on both]

Photographs are primary sources of cultural artifice. They show us glimpses of truth: we can observe what is present and speculate about its significance. While they have a lifelike quality, especially compared to the previous visual forms of painting and sketching, they are still influenced by the lens of the camera, the chosen framing, possible positioning of the subjects, and the source of lighting that fills the scene.

They are not fact. They are not truth. They are merely a representation of something that occurred in the past, but such representations, however possibly flawed, can be collected and inspected aggregately to form a larger picture.

Think of this book as a collection of photographs. Each chapter (a quasi-case study) presents a different facet of people's lives. It is a picture influenced by my own personal lens: life experience, academic background, and social factors. Hopefully the collection of these facets gives us a collage of representations, from which we can discern patterns of larger concepts and gain a loose theoretical understanding of transnational media and cultural exchange as it is happening now.

Primer

Colors and Tints of Meaning: A Glossary for Those Who Don't Know What Anime Is

[Zoom Out]

[Lens: Broad definitions for your average American Joe]

Japanophilia- The love of Japan and its culture, media, history, language, etc. Japanophiles are more concisely defined in the chapter on Otaku Cultural Identity.

Otaku- pronounced oh-TAHK-oo[1] - A word borrowed from Japanese to describe a person who is enthusiastic about Japanese media, particularly anime, manga, cosplay, or video games[2]. The concept of an American Otaku is more developed in the chapter on Otaku Cultural Identity.

Anime- pronounced AH-nih-may or an-IH-may - Cartoons from Japan, either episodic television series or feature length films. Besides their geographic origin,

---

[1] The phonetics estimated here are for these terms as Japanese loanwords in US American English and thus are not authentic Japanese pronunciations but rather the accepted and common American pronunciation.

[2] In Japan, an "otaku" is a fanatic—someone obsessed with something. There are train otaku and jellyfish otaku as well as videogame otaku. This is a book about American culture, so I only use the American version in the pages that follow.

anime differs from US American cartoons in style and content. Stylistically, anime features characters with overly large eyes, long limbs, and fantastic hair colors. Content varies depending on genre, but it is important to establish that Japanese anime is consumed by all demographics in Japan, not just children. Therefore, some of the themes addressed in anime are adult in nature.

Why would someone watch anime and not American cartoons? Motivations change with the times. American children first watched anime in the 1960s simply because it was on the television, having been cheaply sold to US broadcasting companies at the time. In the 1990s, popular anime reflected the changes happening in US American culture after the fall of the Berlin Wall, the societal pressure to distance oneself from communitarianism (communism in all forms) disappeared, and television, particularly children's television, returned to incorporating a team of main characters, rather than the series being focused on the individual protagonist[1]. Additionally, anime slipped into the "Tween" age group which had been previously overlooked as a target demographic. Now in a post 9/11 culture, popular narratives take on darker themes, and

---

[1] US American children's cartoons from this era that were more communitarian than their Spiderman and Superman predecessors include X-Men, Captain Planet, and Teenage Mutant Ninja Turtles.

animes popular here certainly incorporate elements of tragedy and trauma into their stories. In particular, bullying and domestic abuse are often unflinchingly addressed by characters in anime. Other hot topics addressed in anime include globalization as well as the influence of technology on daily life and the human condition.

If anime has been popular in America for so long, why isn't there American anime? There is. <u>Transformers</u>, <u>The Last Airbender</u>, and <u>The Legend of Korra</u> could all be considered US American anime.

Manga- pronounced MAHN-gah or MEYN-guh - Japanese comics, and generally the starting point for Japanese anime. Once again, all ages of Japanese read comics, so the content varies. Authors of manga are "managaka," pronounced mahn-GAH-kah.

J-Drama- A Japanese live-action television drama. Generally, they are the Japanese equivalent of soap opera, targeting a largely adult, female audience (read: housewives).

JRPG- acronym for Japanese role-playing game, a genre of video game of Japanese origin that features a team of (usually playable) main characters, rather than the traditional single protagonist.

Cosplay- Japanese portmanteau of the English words "costume" and "play." Cosplay refers to the art of dressing up as one's favorite anime/manga/video game character. "Cosplayers" are those who create and wear these elaborate and painstakingly created costumes.

Con- Short for "convention," an event organized around a central topic or theme. **Anime cons**, therefore, are gatherings of people to celebrate and enjoy anime. Throughout this book, I use "anime con" as an umbrella term for any con which promotes Japanese or Asian culture. Anime is the current focal point of these cons, thus the reduction of the name. Anime cons are more thoroughly addressed in the chapter "An Oversimplified Cultural History."

Other Terms Employed:

Kanji- pronunciation KAHN-gee- Japanese characters. Romanized words are phonetic approximations of Japanese words. For example, "manga" is the Romanized word for Japanese comics, and " 漫画 " are the kanji for the same word.

Fandom- The subculture and community of fans of a particular franchise, media, or art form. **Fan fiction** refers to fan-created stories within the favored media, narrative, television show, etc. The definition of fan fiction is explored more in the Introduction to Fan Fiction chapter.

Other terms are defined when introduced within the chapters, either at length in paragraph form or briefly in footnotes.

Setting the Scene: An Oversimplified Cultural History

The next few chapters will inspect of the mixture of US American and Japanese cultures as seen in the cultural artifacts (media, film, comics, songs) and cultural institutions (anime cons.)
If we seek to discern the framing of this cultural mélange, then we need a brief historical overlook to view the context of cultural blending in the US.

[Setting 1: US American culture]

[Lens: How Americans view themselves]

Mixing Pot vs. Salad Bowl Cultural Ideas

Many Americans learn in primary school that the nation is a "Melting Pot" of peoples. The metaphor relates how the cultural identities of incumbent immigrants are assimilated into the national identity, which is also impacted by the addition. The cultural identities "melt" like ingredients into a soup, maintaining many original tastes but also adopting more strongly the flavor of the base itself-the American national identity. The "broth" is also affected by the inclusion of these ingredients. This cultural idea has been part of how Americans define their culture for over a century. More recently, and particularly after the civil rights movement of the 1960s, an alternative idea of a "salad bowl" has become popular in academic conversations about cultural identity. In this model, different "ingredients" or cultural identities exist separately and juxtaposed to each other, still maintaining their unique identity while being an active part of the whole.

Anime Cons Overview

[Zoom In: Setting 2: Con culture]

[Lens: Source of this information is from oral histories recounted at mostly East Coast cons and from dialogues with long-time anime con goers/staff.]

In the 1970s and 1980s, science fiction conventions often incorporated anime into their programming. Despite the fact that offering anime gave the conventions an additional draw to their membership, anime fans at sci-fi cons were often ostracized, and their viewing rooms were often placed in an out-of-the-way corner or off a rear corridor of the venue. This act of "othering" is a common phenomenon in the crafting of group identity: we are this, because we aren't that. Exclusion, therefore, is an exercise of community building. At sci-fi cons, anime was included for drawing on similar themes (technology, robotics, etc.) but excluded for being outside the relative norm.

As anime became more popular and their isolated viewing rooms filled, many of these anime-fan black sheep came together and split off the parent sci-fi convention to form their own, smaller but independent anime cons. The 1990s saw an anime boom as Sailor Moon and Dragon Ball Z (and later Pokémon) were shown in major network/non-cable channels. These shows' popularity was bolstered by syndication on the Cartoon Network programming block "Toonami." In anime con culture, the "Toonami generation" refers to this group of anime fans who were introduced to the art form from these popular 90s shows.

Anime cons have since become an edifice in US popular culture. The largest cons have over 30,000 attendees, and almost every city has an anime con on the East Coast. According to animecons.com, there are more than 150 anime cons in the US scheduled for 2015.

I posit that these cons are gathering points for a unique cultural identity, the Otaku, which is a third cultured mix of Japanese and US American cultures. (This idea is explored more in the chapter on Otaku Cultural Identity and in the chapter "Are Otaku Globalization's First Children?") The Anime Con serves as a home-base for these third-cultured individuals.

A noticeable majority of anime conventions are education-oriented nonprofit organizations, and these cons are hosted by lay-people who often have no professional event planning experience. The staffers are volunteers, who put in hundreds of hours of planning and execution to pull off one to three day events. The largest East Coast convention, Otakon, is a three-day event with over seven hundred volunteer staff hosting more than thirty thousand members. While it is a multimillion dollar event, the only paid staff are the outsourced accountants and the lawyers of the non-profit Otakorp incorporation.

All anime cons follow the same structure: con-goers can meet famous Japanese and American guests, attend lectures, concerts, dances, and workshops, as well as buy licensed and unique fanwork wares in the ("dealers room" and "artist alley") markets. Anime conventions represent the best of both Japanese and US American cultures: Japanese ingenuity and embracing of novelty with US work ethic, Japanese collectivity and team work with US ambition and self-motivation, Japanese fanaticism and American inclusivity. The actualization of this mixing and converging of cultures is examined at length in the chapter "Are Otaku Globalization's first Children?"

Additional Notes:

- In many ways, an anime con functions as a micropolis, a temporary village for the Otaku culture to reside, complete with markets (dealers rooms and artist alleys in exhibition halls), elected governing individuals (con chairs and other leadership), arts (performances, showings of anime music videos that are made by local Otaku, and licensed viewings of Japanese media) education (panels), lodging (hotels adjacent to convention centers), and community-building exercises (workshops). It is important to note that cons promote both primary works of Japanese culture (anime, music, and their creators) and secondary works of Otaku culture: the wares in Artist Alleys and beautiful and carefully wrought anime music videos in which Otaku blend anime-source video with (often US American) pop songs.

- Located in the Addendum: Discard Pile are unedited, un-betaed notes on Regional Differences for Anime Cons and the Feasibility of an Ameri-Con Overseas.

Establishing Shot: The Making of a "Cool Japan[1]" in Mainstream America

[Zoom Out: Mainstream America and Japanese Culture]

[Lens: Quasi-objective point of view of US cultural changes, due to my absence from the States August 2008 through January 2010, while I held academic fellowships France, Germany, and China]

"We are programming your websites, making your senior executives look smart, and getting into your schools for free! That's right, raise the bar! ... [We're] bigger than Japanese in rap songs, and yoga!" from Beau Sia's "Asian Invasion"

While I was working as an English Teaching assistant in an upper-crust, exclusive French high school, one of my students asked "In France, learning about the USA and studying English is cool. What country do Americans think is cool?"

In that moment, the idea of Japan flashed in my mind, but I responded with a generic "no particular nation is favored by ALL Americans. Many enjoy British TV, but there are many other groups of

---

[1] "Cool Japan" is both an NHK (that is, Japan's ABC or CBS) television show on Japanese culture and, from what I hear, a governmental initiative to promote Japanese culture abroad.

Americans that like films and media from other countries as well."

When I returned to the US a year and a half later, I found it profoundly altered. Besides the obvious cultural changes due to the recession which occurred in entirety while I was abroad, there were many striking developments in US-Japan media exchanges and relations.

Firstly, Asians were dramatically more present in cable advertising. They were portrayed as well-educated, high-achieving, affluent individuals. Such roles, in my memory, were much more exclusively played by whites pre-2008 (the year I left.) Asians were the new face of US American affluence, and any high-tech, high-luxury product or service employed an Asian in their ad campaign. (This idea only became more salient, and three years later American beauty ideals reflected the trending idolization of Asians. One cable television channel ran a story exposing that all [non-Asian] American men prefer Asian women to those of other ethnic backgrounds, according to a study of over two million people on the dating app Are You Interested[1].)

---

[1] Comedienne Kristina Wong was a guest speaker on the news story, and posted the clip to her YouTube profile. Accessed October 25, 2014. https://www.youtube.com/watch?v=rmH0XaG4deA "Why Everyone Wants to Date Asian Babes with Kristina Wong Asian Fever".

Secondly, yaoi could be found in bookstores in even the Bible Belt. Yaoi is a genre of gay romantic comic books that target a straight women audience. I was shocked to see any such material in a bookstore in the most conservative region of the US, never mind a large and diverse quantity of it.

Thirdly, Americans had started to become markedly more communitarian. Hyper-individualism was at its height in the 80s and early 90s, but, due to many political and pluralizing influences, had been on a decline[1]. A primary influence, in my opinion, was the fallout from Robert Putnam's <u>Bowling Alone</u>[2] and higher education's response--shifting their profile of the ideal student. Community involvement became increasingly important in addition to academic achievement for any college-bound student. There was now an institutional impetus for individuals to be more community-minded.

A secondary influence playing a role in the move away from hyper-individualism came from Japanese

---

[1] After the resolution of the Cold War and the fall of the Berlin Wall, the need for communism-paranoia disappeared; however this does not necessitate a shift to a more communitarian society.

[2] Putnam's nonfiction expose argued that Americans were becoming disconcertingly more socially isolated, as reflected in the disappearance of bowling leagues. The text was hugely popular in university and college faculty and administrations, and shortly thereafter we saw a shift of the ideal student having strong test scores and a high GPA to one who also was involved in their community and held leadership positions in afterschool activities. While correlation does not beget causation, the timing of these two events is suspect.

trade. Japanese videogames saw a boom in the 1990s: starting with the popularity of the Nintendo and Super Nintendo home gaming systems, and spreading to home computer video game play with the booming popularity of Final Fantasy VII. Japanese videogames, particularly the popular and influential JRPGs, in which one plays a protagonist who is a part of a team that uses each member's talents to achieve common goals, gave young adults an alternative view of how superheroes function: the hero doesn't always save the day by himself, but rather heads a team of unique individuals with different talents who together solve the problem.

A few years later (2010-2014) we see this same shift in films and television shows. These media before focused on one protagonist with perhaps two supporting characters. Now it is commonplace for narratives to incorporate five or more highly developed characters. Part of this change is certainly thanks to Joss Whedon, but JRPG influence remains a viable contribution to the evolution of American consumers. For example, the Kung Fu Panda franchise not only features an Asian story setting, but also integrates and focuses on the team mentality in addition to using wide-angle videogame-like camera shots.

These instances of Japanese media influencing US media paved the way for more distinct inclusions of Japanese culture in US franchises. More examples are inspected in greater depth in the following chapters.

Additional Notes:

- Brief overview of US American cultural identity, as reported by BBC: http://news.bbc.co.uk/2/hi/americas/4931534.stm
- I hear Henry Jenkins has many works along these lines (i.e. participatory culture, culture convergence, etc.) He is highly recommended to anyone with interest along these lines.
- Discarded notes from this chapter on page 121 in the Addendum: Is Japanese culture "cool"?
- Beau Sia's "Asian Invasion" https://www.youtube.com/watch?v=diNLPGHZbGM

Matting: Japanophile, Otaku, and Weeaboo: a Cultural Identity Spectrum

Since 1995, media from foreign countries can more easily permeate US American line of sight. With a few clicks on the Internet, we can find or are shown, foreign music videos, films, and blogs. This has led to an increased diversity of popular media, especially music, penetrating the American market. (For example, Moldova's O-Zone "Dragostea din Tei" in 2004, 2012 South Korea's PSY "Oppa Gagnam Style," and 2013 Norway's Ylvis "The Fox.") Cuisine, fashion, and video games have also been heavily impacted by the influence of globalization and increased internationalization as trends more and more easily flow across national borders.

Even though Japan and America fought a war during the first half of the twentieth century, by the turn of the millennium relations had much improved due to the Marshall Plan's legacy and increased trade between the two countries. Astro Boy, which was shown on major broadcast networks in the 1960s, garnered the first generation of anime fans here in the US. It is interesting to note that a majority of the viewers of the show were unaware of its Japanese origin. For the children who tuned in, it was merely a cartoon. By the 1980s, trade relations were strong between the two countries, and the US media included non-demonized Japanese and Asian characters in pop culture ("Domo Arigato, Mister Roboto" and Gedde Watanabe's roles in <u>Sixteen Candles</u> and <u>UHF</u>). American teenagers watched the anime <u>Speed Racer</u> (this time knowing it was Japanese) and intellectuals were touting their highbrow culture by dining on sushi.

The 1990s saw a pro-Japan boom with the tween popularity cresting on <u>Sailor Moon</u>, <u>Dragon Ball Z</u>, and <u>Pokémon</u>. For the first time, we saw non-English, foreign canon franchise products infiltrating US markets en masse: Dragon Ball Z manga (Japanese style comic books) being sold nationwide in Books-A-Million chain stores, Sailor Moon alarm clocks and accessories being sold at Claire's Boutiques, and VHS tapes of Pokémon at Toys-R-Us. Armed with dial-up Internet and Windows 95 Home PCs, children who watched these shows were also enabled to learn more about Japanese culture during their formative years.

As a Sailor Moon fan of the 90s, I was greatly impressed by the widespread geographic dispersion of fans, as well as how many were creative in their enthusiasm. I remember spending hours on image-hosting websites, crafting my own GeoCities fansite with pages dedicated to each character, and slowly downloading gifs and jpegs of art and midis of music. I even downloaded and printed out a Sailor Moon-themed cookbook, and I still to this day use that recipe for

Snickerdoodles, a cookie unheard of in my corner of the world[1].

For some fans, these shows were just a passing phase. Many, however, would continue their love of Japanese anime and manga. Their appreciation would grow to include other art forms: fashion and high fashion (aka cosplay,) videogames, music, and cuisine. These individuals would become Otaku. Their love of this foreign culture impacting their lives.

Otakudom is different for each individual. Some choose a particular series--e.g. Sailor Moon or Naruto--then grow and develop alongside the protagonists every stage of their childhood, adolescence, and adulthood through the fifty-plus books in the franchise. Western narrative lacks these long-haul stories, with the notable exception of trendsetting Harry Potter. Other Otakus adopt a certain art form, such as cosplay or JRPGs, spend hours learning the details and nuance of those forms, and design their own creations after the Japanese style.

Otakus' love also drives them to spend time/money on Japanese goods and culture rather those of the USA. Spending time being immersed, if only indirectly, in Japanese culture primes Otakus to become even more involved in that foreign lifestyle. When they meet other Otakus at cons, this foreign influence is only

---

[1] This is an example of post-geographic acculturation, a concept discussed at length in the chapter of Otaku as Globalization's Children.

reinforced as they are given both social and marketplace trade opportunities to acquire more knowledge and cultural artifacts. Simply put, loving one element of Japanese culture enables individuals to love more of it, eventually becoming Otaku, and cons only snowball this appreciation.

At a convention in 2013, I was introduced to the idea of a "weeaboo." For the Otaku community, weeaboos are people who seek to constantly immerse themselves in Japanese culture, despite living in the USA, in a conscious and often pretentiously declared attempt to "become Japanese," forsaking their own native culture. Most Otaku view weeaboos with contempt, especially since weeaboos are generally overenthusiastic young people going through a phase, but also because of a quiet understanding that these individuals see Japan through an extremely exotified lens. Another point of contention lies in weeaboos' propensity to value the small tangent of culture to which they've been exposed as more important than the whole of Japanese culture. The culture is diminished and compressed to an item to acquire or a status to achieve rather than a living, breathing, multi-faceted set of ideas and mores.

When I heard the idea of weeaboo in the Otaku community, I was happy to see a distinction being made between fans who enthusiastically engage the culture and those who simply exotify it. The practice of exclusion also makes for a tighter community, and weeaboos are possibly the best party to exclude. Rather than dividing along race or gender lines like many other subcultures, Otakus are actively excluding people who make unhealthy decisions and ignorant judgements.

On the other side of the spectrum, we have Japanophiles. Japanophiles number far fewer than the Otaku population. These individuals have a culturally relativistic appreciation for Japanese culture. They understand the worth of this foreign culture and seek to learn more about it. They study the language and read Japanese texts in the original form. They become East Asia studies minors (or majors)[1]. They apply to the prestigious and highly exclusive JET Programme in order to teach English in Japan for two years. They learn about Japan not only through its cultural exports, but also through academic texts. They explore not only its culture, but also its economy, politics, and history.

Now we have a spectrum of engagement with Japanese culture, ranging from a culturally relativistic point of view to that of extreme exotification. The following chapters provide snapshots of ways Japanese culture makes inroads into US American culture through case-studies of different specific pieces of art, most of which have been released in the US over the past twelve months. These snapshots are brief inspections of the

---

[1] Recommended listening: Beau Sia's "Asian Invasion"

intermingling of two cultures on US soil. Polish, nuance, and development of these depictions have been, to some degree, sacrificed to immediacy of publishing these commentaries, interpretations, and critiques. The flow of media goes ever on, and by the time this book is published many of the artifacts examined will already be well on their way of being obsolete examples of pop culture.

Additional notes found in the Addendum: Discard Pile:
- Why do anime characters have big eyes? p.125
- Why do we like anime? p. 125

Snapshots

Dark Pasts, Bright Futures: Reconciling WWII Human Rights Violations through Friendship

Art shows us who we think we were, who we are, and who we are on the brink of becoming.

It is a common point of frustration and complaint among young American scholars in Germany that the Nazi regime is erased from public discourse and apparently public memory. I remember quite clearly, one day after a lecture in my DAF[1] Twentieth Century German History course at Universität Stuttgart, a diatribe among my foreign exchange colleagues as we walked back to the S-bahn. One of the young men was incensed by the way the professor had glazed over direct questions about those hateful, heartless Nazis.

The rant is familiar to any American holding even a passing acquaintance with modern day German society. My mind drifted to a previous semester's reading while still in the United States: Harald Welzer and several others had tackled this cognitive distancing with a book entitled "Opa war kein Nazi[2]" or "Granddad

---

[1] Deustche als Fremdsprache: Courses taught in German but in more simplistic language for non-native speakers.

[2] Opa war kein Nazi. Nationalsozialismus und Holocaust im

wasn't a Nazi" in 2003. My lingering impression of that work was the enormity of reconciling the image of your loving grandpa who spoils you with someone who may have committed atrocities or at least turned a blind eye to them.

Such past hurts are often the deepest. How do we tend to them?

Memorial Day Sunday, May 25, 2014: Christ of the Hills Church, Hot Springs Village, Arkansas

After applauding for the men and women who had served in the military, the congregation of this Methodist church began singing a patriotic hymn, and my eyes wander over the people around me as the familiar words tumble out of my mouth with rote certainty.

Some of these individuals were members of the G.I. Generation and fought in World War II. I had recently viewed The Railway Man in the theater, a film starring Colin Firth and Nicole Kidman. Based on an autobiography, the protagonist Eric Lomax had suffered inhumane indenture and torture at a Japanese prisoner of war camp. The Japanese beat the prisoners. The Japanese treated the prisoners as slaves. The primary Japanese antagonist water boards a young Lomax on screen.

Familiengedächtnis by Harald Welzer, Sabine Moller, Karoline Tschuggnall, Olaf Jensen, and Torsten Koch. Published in 2012 by Tisher in Frankfurt, Germany.

Lomax's psyche was shattered by what he experienced in the War.

Much of the frame of the story takes place in the years after the war as the survivors carry on with their lives. One of Lomax's friends and fellow comrade from the FEPOW[1] camp, described their common struggle with battle fatigue:[2]

When we surrendered, the Japs said we weren't men. Real men would kill themselves or die of shame, but we said "No. We'll live for revenge." But we didn't. No, we don't live. We're miming in the choir. We can't love. We can't sleep. We're an army of ghosts.

Stellan Skarsgård as Finlay,
<u>The Railway Man</u> *(2012)*

Hatred and revenge tear at the minds of the survivors of the war. They don't escape the memory of the inhumanity of man. Tragically, this story is not unfamiliar to the American audience. While The Railway Man is a film based in autobiography, other permutations of the same story have come to the silver screen with a perhaps disturbing regularity.

---

[1] FEPOW for "Far East Prisoners of War" is a common acronym to US and British veterans and communities.

[2] Psychological difficulty with re-acclimating to civilian life after the traumatic experience of military warfare. "Shell shock" described the same disorder for returning soldiers after WWI, and nowadays we refer to it a Post-Traumatic Stress Disorder.

In 1983, David Bowie (well known to my generation for handsomely challenging a young girl to traverse "through dangers untold and hardships unnumbered" to protect her baby brother[1]) and Ryuichi Sakamoto (well known to American Otaku for his breathtakingly beautiful orchestral compositions and exquisite piano playing) starred in the Japanese-British film <u>Merry Christmas, Mr. Lawrence</u>. Based on the novel <u>The Seed and the Sower</u> by Laurens van der Post, this film even-handedly shows the psychologically destructive force of war on both captor and captive in a WWII Japanese prisoner of war camp. In the film, all men are oppressed by the experience, reducing them to their basic emotions. Sex, shame, violence, hunger, grief, self-righteousness, and survival are all touched upon at a disorienting pace. Once again, the white POWs struggle with the Japanese concept of honor and shame in the face of human rights violations: the trailer remarks, "They were all honorable men, but oh what deeds could be done in the name of honor." This film once again showed the American audience atrocities committed by the Japanese on Allied forces, but it wasn't the first major motion picture to do so.

---

[1] Bowie starred opposite a young Jennifer Connelly in Jim Henson's "The Labyrinth" in 1986. Despite underperforming at the box office, the film has since gathered an underground cult following, especially among Gen Xers who watched it during their childhood.

The Bridge On the River Kwai premiered in 1957, won seven Academy Awards, and is a considered classic in American film. Based on a novel of the same name by Frenchman Pierre Boulle, a white officer played by Alec Guinness pridefully bears starvation and entrapment in an enclosed cage as he refuses to give up the rights guaranteed to himself and his men in the Geneva Convention. In a most fantastic and exaggerated telling of the goings-on in labor camps, the men prisoners arrive at the camp whistling a cheerful tune, and at the end of the movie, depart in the same manner. The captive Lieutenant Colonel bests the Japanese Camp Commandant through pure stubbornness in the face of darkness and death.

These three films, while the chronological first two are based on novels and the third based on autobiography, are remarkably similar. All three are set in prisoner of war camps. The Railway Man is set in a construction camp for the Burma railway, which is the same railway to traverse the bridge over the river Kwai in that film. Despite the fact that Merry Christmas, Mr. Lawrence mostly takes place in the hospital wing of a labor camp, human rights violations are there too a reality for the captives.

These three films touch on our legacy of pain from World War II. Our past hurts are the deepest. Their scars invisible, hidden to the casual everyday observation, only to be drawn out in these works of art.

The men who lived these circumstances survive still. How do we honor their sacrifices? How do we acknowledge their suffering with dignity? How do we show them respect, but by looking unflinchingly at what they have endured for our sakes? For our freedom? For our prosperity?

How do we respond to the horrors committed on us in the past? One answer to this unanswerable question is to acknowledge and remember the horrors we committed on others. In 2011 I first heard George Takei[1] drumming up interest in his self-proclaimed "legacy project"—a musical reflecting his childhood in a Japanese internment camp in Arkansas, the ruins of which lie some 150 miles to the southeast of Hot Springs Village. Growing up on the East side of the United States, I have no memory of learning about Japanese internment in my primary education. My first acquaintance with it was in a human rights course in college, and I gained more awareness from visiting museums in the San Francisco area when I briefly lived there in the winter of 2005[2]. The barbarity of our own

[1] George Takei is an American actor of Japanese descent who played the role of Hikaru Sulu in 1960 hit television series Star Trek. His visibility and influence resurged in the 2010s as his social media posts became virally popular.

[2] I also have a small memory of the Supreme Court case Korematsu v. United States, which questioned the constitutionality of the executive order which mandated internment of possible citizen spies without proof of illegal action, being briefly alluded to in an episode of the television series The West Wing, but it is a brief remark in a

government towards its citizens hovered in the periphery of my mind, but I was all too aware, then, of my peers' ignorance of this truth.

Now, Americans are much more familiar with this uncomfortable part of our past, and, thanks to Takei, interment is in our society's consciousness. The latest, and perhaps largest, incorporation of internment into our popular culture was season 3B of MTV's most popular current young adult television show, Teen Wolf. Running January through March of 2014, this season's story arc incorporates elements of Japanese culture and folklore into the previously established Western supernatural myth structure. A mainstream, young adult audience was presented with the world of oni (Japanese demons), kitsune (trickster fox spirits), yakuza (mobsters), and more. This introduction makes future stylistic or cultural influences from the land of the Rising Sun more *accessible* and *familiar* to them. Furthermore, the crux of the season hangs on events that occurred at a World War II Japanese internment camp in California. "The Fox and the Wolf" (episode twenty-one of season two) is an episode conducted almost entirely in flashback, showing the young viewers the hardships endured by displaced Japanese at the hands of often corrupt if not unnecessarily violent military personnel. At one point, the white captors steal much-needed

---

quick repartee between two characters.

medicine from the internment camp to sell on the black market. For the first time in American television, historical human rights violations by representatives of the US government are presented to a teenage audience. These young people will grow up not only with a more realistic image of our country but also more mature patriotism towards it.

Teen Wolf is not the only piece of popular culture that has ridden the wave of awareness of Japanese internment. On Independence Day of this year (2014), the edutainment giant TED released an article listing ten pop culture artworks reflecting this dark chapter of America's past. Perhaps the most surprising entry is a song written by a former member of the band Linkin Park telling the story of a family being in an internment camp.[1]

The main antagonist of the aforementioned season of Teen Wolf is an ancient evil spirit possessing a teenage boy. The spirit wreaks havoc on the community, and "draws its power from pain and tragedy, strife and chaos." In several occasions, it goads characters to draw from past hurts and anger to break into violence. This spirit in many ways symbolizes the destructive force of hatred in societies. "Sometime the hating has to stop,"

---

[1] "What Pop Culture can Teach us About Japanese Internment" by Kate Torgovnick May, July 4, 2014, on Ideas.Ted.Com: accessed October 31, 2014. http://ideas.ted.com/2014/07/04/what-pop-culture-can-teach-us-about-japanese-internment/

says Eric Lomax, as he pieces his life back together, confronting the revenants of his traumatic memories from World War II, emerging from the experience in friendship with the Japanese soldier who was his captor in the POW camp.

How do we address the horrors of the past? Reconciliation is the hardest part of conflict resolution. Honesty is not easy. It is not easy to remember the wrongs we have visited on others while someone perpetrates atrocity. Dialogue is not easy. Winston Churchill once said, "Courage is what it takes to stand up and speak; courage is also what it takes to sit down and listen." The way to honor the pain of the past is to strive not to be inhumane in retaliation to inhumanity, but rather to seek the humanity in every person, no matter his/her actions.

Addendum, December 3, 2014:

The American people is in pain. Once again, we see structural violence committed against our citizens. These are dark times, and there is no easy solution. I recall ranting at a very patient fellow anime-con lecturer this past October. I wished that the Tuskegee Syphilis Study would be as commonly known as Japanese internment. Sadly, this large human rights violation by the US Public Health Service remains in obscurity. I still hope for resolution. If there is a lesson to be learned in the improved public image of Asian Americans from 1940s to today, perhaps we can apply similar efforts to how we view other minorities, shaping our society to be fairer, more inclusive, and less violent against those who do not share the same physical appearance as the majority.

Additional Notes:
- A soundtrack of this chapter can be found here: http://8tracks.com/softpowerpunch-428/merry-christmas-mr-railway-man

US and Japanese Grassroots Writing:
An Introduction to Fan Fiction

In Japan they have doujinshi. Doujinshi refers to self-published creative works, usually comics or fiction, and this type of media is a long-established, lucrative way for artists to start and fund their careers. Doujinshi divides into two subtypes: original work and work that emulates or parodies popular franchises.

In the USA we have fan fiction, which has slowly been building over the past half century. Newcomers to the fan fiction ("fanfic") scene have trouble distinguishing fan fiction from other well established works of parody and re-imagination. Is Bridget Jones's Diary a fan fiction of Pride and Prejudice? Is John Gardner's Grendel a fanfic of Beowulf?

Two years ago, I would have explained that they were not, due to the fact that, outside of emulation, fanfic's defining characteristic is a grassroots level of distribution. Historically fan fiction was produced for small communities: homemade fanzine[1] anthologies of local fans' musings of "What if this episode went this

---

[1] "Fanzine" is a portmanteau of "Fan" and "magazine." The 1980s and early 90s in particular saw a boom of home or Kinko-made "zines," publications by groups of enthusiastic groups of fans or very productive individuals. Fanzines from the Star Trek community in the 1970s were some of the earliest forms of "fan fiction," in one meaning of the term.

way…" or "What if these two characters were secretly dating…"

While fan fiction writers used and continue to use the structures presented in the main franchises, the content was and is their own. Fan fiction engages a long list of topics often deemed as inappropriate, taboo, or otherwise unable to turn a profit on the mass market. Gender and sexual orientation issues are the most popular dialogues presented fan fiction, but also race and class are addressed. Of course, these four subjects *are* addressed in popular media; however, fanfic regularly engages with these topics in a raw, often brutally honest and direct manner that would be impermissible in mainstream media, as it would lower ratings and commercial success. (This idea is more explored in the Yaoi and Slash snapshot chapter starting on page 51.)

With the arrival of the personal computer and household Internet in the 1990s, fans had a new mode of connection. Writers could create and publish a fanfic on a personal website, and others could find it using search engines. 1998 saw the establishment of fanfiction.net, which became a hub and model for the sharing of user-created content.

If we fast forward[1] to today, the newest nonprofit hub of fanfiction, ArchiveOfOurOwn.org, has over one million fanworks. This site recently completed[2] a

---

[1] Yes, proud member of Gen Y here who grew up with VHS tapes, thus the "fast forwarding."

fundraising event (a red banner across the top of their pages) and saw the fulfillment of its $70,000 goal within forty-eight hours. The fundraiser continued for its dedicated one week and garnered the nonprofit parent Organization for Transformative Works over $164,000 in that short time.

In addition to growth of participation and distribution of fanfic, this new form has also evolved in narrative mode relative to media types available to fan creators. Fans create Facebook and Twitter accounts in the names of their favorite characters and "role play" conversations, creating a dialogue-text fanwork. Non-collaborative creation still remains popular on networking sites, as seen in the growth of fanfic on DeviantArt.com and Tumblr. Linked to an Archive of Our Own page, one fan fiction creator even made a digital magazine devoted to one fictional work of the Teen Wolf fandom, bringing the mode of fan fiction creation back to its earlier roots.

Cultural gatekeepers[1] (the big five publishers of the literary world, and the major networks of the television sphere) have sat up and paid attention and, increasingly, homage to this movement in society towards fan engagement of popular media. This year, fans have been rewarded with meta-episodes of BBC's

---

[2] Fall 2004: http://archiveofourown.org/admin_posts/1775

[1] Also academia has been paying attention. Henry Jenkins and increasing amount of universities and academic journals.

Sherlock[1] and the CW's Supernatural[2] that directly address fans *in canon narrative*. With the popular success of Cassandra Clare's The Mortal Instruments, a re-purposed Drarry[3] Harry Potter fan fiction, and Fifty Shades of Grey, an erotic reimagining of the characters from Twilight, many publishers are eagerly looking for the next fanfic to become a popular sensation. Indeed, Amazon has created its Kindle Worlds, a branch of official fan fiction publishing, to capitalize on fanfic's popularity.

Fan fiction is no longer an underground, micro-level creative medium. This brings us back to the question of "What makes it a fanfic?" Many would argue that it is more pluralistic than established franchises of media. This is a continuation of the Millennial idea that the Internet is a great, global, democratizing instrument. Yes, fanfic is very engaging of gender dialogue omitted from mainstream franchises; however, this does not make for a wholly democratic medium. While the ability to write and publish fanfic is democratically distributed, the agency and support structure necessary to have a

---

[1] Season 3 episode 1, #SherlockLives showing fan communities coming together and hypothesizing how Sherlock could have survived the Reichenbach Fall. US Premier Jan 19, 2014

[2] The 200th episode aired on Nov 11, 2014, was entitled "Fan Fiction," and featured a fan fiction writer who adapted her work into a musical of "Supernatural," including the protagonists and main characters of the television show.

[3] Harry Potter/Draco Malfoy slash fan fiction, i.e. a story that involves the romantic relationship of those two characters.

successful fanfic[1] or even fulfilling experience is limited. In simpler terms, anyone can write fanfic, but the most successful fanfic writers are white, upper-middle class or upper class individuals.

Overall, fan fiction does allow individuals en masse to engage, interact, and emote with popular franchises on individualized and intimate levels. The growth of fan fiction in US American culture is a win/win: consumers are able to tailor narratives to their own needs and desires, and producers are granted access to previously unreached communities, gaining the ability to permeate these subcultures through such grassroots adaptations.

---

[1] Fanart and cosplay are even worse with direct disparaging of minorities or those with less resources to create an expensive product.

Disappearing Women: Tracing Femininity and Women's Gender Roles through TV and Film Media in the US and Japan

In America,
Books teach us how to imagine,
TV media how to interact,
Music how to feel,
and Videogames how to think.

I first gave this talk in January of 2014. I was grappling with the multifaceted and often oppositional if not antipodal portrayals of and messages about women in visual media, especially those which featured female protagonists and feminine target audience. After ruminating on the idea, I saw the emergence of three categories divided along the lines of how the protagonist dealt with the idea of femininity and her struggle with her feminine identity. I saw a lessening in the depiction of women's physical attributes/identity, while the mental and emotional side of women grew stronger. Let's trace this disappearance.

Step One: Breakthrough Women Breaking

In this category, the strong female protagonist, with whom the female target audience identifies, struggles with doing it all, and suffers a break--physical

or emotional--from overexertion. The character tries to
balance personal and familial life with professional
ambition, and something has to give. In Japanese media,
we see several examples of this ranging in popularity
and across demographics. Japanese media targeting
female audiences are split into two demographics:
shoujo, which targets girls ages eight to sixteen, and
josei, which targets women ages seventeen to fifty-five[1].
Examples of shoujo media with this theme include The
Wallflower[2], a story of a woman who hides away her
femininity in her pursuit and love of all things horror.
Also Kaichou wa Maid Sama[3] and Hana Yori Dango[4]
(the plot of which has been popular for over two
decades) both feature high school-aged female
protagonists who, due to working jobs, having active
after-school lives, and studying, suffer exhaustion to the
degree of hospitalization or at least need medical care to
heal. For the josei demographic, we have the series
Pride, where a woman has a good career and supportive
friends, but lacks romantic development, eventually

---

[1] Other ages are identified aggregately with their male counterparts,
either as "children" or "retired persons".

[2] Popular in the US and Japan. In Japan, the manga began in 2000, anime
ran 2006-2007, drama 2010.

[3] Popular in Europe, especially France, and Japan. In Japan, the manga
started in 2000, anime 2006-2007, drama 2010,

[4] Popular throughout Asia, inspiring manga-based anime and j-drama in
Japan, as well as dramas in Hong Kong, South Korea (2009), Taiwan
(2001-2002), Indonesia (2002,) and Mainland China. In Japan, manga was
published 1992-2003, anime 1996-97, film 1995, drama 2005-07.

descending into a relationship with domestically violent partner; <u>Anego</u>, in which the career-woman protagonist outright says her professional life gets in the way of her securing dates; and <u>Gokusen</u>, where the female protagonist must hide her familial life to keep her dream job as a teacher of high school students.

In US media, the examples abound. With the narrow category of female protagonists who sacrifice personal/familial life for their professional development, there are major motion pictures such as <u>The Devil Wears Prada</u> (2006), <u>The Iron Lady</u> (2011), and <u>Zero Dark Thirty</u> (2012). Widen the scope of the dilemma and even more popular films fit this category: In <u>Mona Lisa Smile</u> (2003), the female characters are presented with a choice of professional (academic) ambition or familial life, but no depiction of a balance of the two is portrayed. <u>Dreamgirls</u>' (2006) empowered women protagonists could have good careers or good family lives (i.e. good husbands) but not both. The first three installments of the <u>Twilight</u> saga (2008-2012), in an artistic twist of this theme, set up the choice of financial security or family (i.e. the ability to bear children.) Even the acclaimed <u>Frozen</u> (2013) featured a female protagonist who, for 95% of the film, had hide her emotive side (often seen as a feminine trait) in order to be a good ruler.

With all these examples of women having to give up part of themselves in order to be successful, are we addressing the struggles of women or teaching our daughters that they must *adapt* themselves in order to survive in a man's world?

Step Two: Feminine Bodies, Masculine Masks[1]

Our next category has fewer examples, but they are still a salient contribution to the self-image of women in the two countries. If women must give up part of themselves to be successful in a man's world, then why not simply have it all by disguising themselves as men? Japanese examples which have seen international success include Hana Kimi (aka Hanazakari no Kimitachi E[2] and Ouran High School Host Club[3], which both feature female protagonists who must cross dress and pretend to be male students in order to accomplish their goals[4]. This theme ping pongs around Asia[5], with

---

[1] Title of this section is after Fanon's Peau Noire, Masques Blanches

[2] The manga ran 1996-2004, the 2007 drama was so successful that it was remade a mere three years later with a new cast but same set. The remake features a new subplot twists in which the school is facing financial difficulty, explaining the poor condition of the buildings and interiors.

[3] The manga ran from 2002-2010. The 2006 anime saw huge popularity both in Japan and the US, leading to the creation of a J-drama in 2011 and a live-action feature in 2012.

[4] Ouran High School Host Club fans may dispute this claim, referencing that Haruhi merely doesn't correct others' incorrect assumption of her gender due her indifference of which gender she is perceived to be. The *message* of the show, however, still stands that her being in male dress helps her on her journey to succeed in school life.

[5] 2004 saw the publishing of ½ Prince, a Taiwanese Manhwa comic in which a female protagonist is granted the chance to be a male character in

Hana Kimi being remade in Korea, Taiwan, and Indonesia. The Korean television series <u>You're Beautiful</u>, about a girl posing as her twin brother to be in a boy band, was remade in Japan and Taiwan. Even mainland China sees a version of this theme with <u>My Bratty Princess</u> (2005) in which a princess disguises herself as a ruffian to take down nobles a notch and redistribute their gambled money to the poor.

Western examples of cross-dressing female protagonists are fewer, but just as impactful[1]. There are many permutations of and allusions to Shakespeare's <u>Twelfth Night</u>, and even Disney has a princess who cross dresses to find a "reflection of herself" that she feels is authentic (<u>Mulan</u>). The best playwright of the English language and the second largest broadcasting company in the USA certainly influence our culture on a massive scale.

Now we have seen female role models needing to pretend to be men, outright, in order to qualify for a possibility of success. With this even more broken self-image, it is clear to discern the need for women to completely put away their female identity in order to

---

an MMORPG, in which all players' avatars must be representative of their birth-assigned genders. ½ Prince became an underground international success.

[1] Including Queen Christina, a 1933 film in which Greta Garbo cross-dresses as a young hunter boy to escape the pressures of ruling. Interestingly, this film satisfies the Bechdel test.

exist in certain spheres. This sets the stage for our third category.

Step Three: Gender Identity Displacement

When women and girls are confronted with role models that are only destructive to their psyche, the simplest solution is, oddly enough, to become men. Imagine parts of your identity as building blocks: one for assertiveness, another for demureness, one for pride, another for humility, one for social capability, another for gestures and physical communication skills, and so on. Some of these traits, society teaches us, are rewarded in men and others are rewarded in women. In this final category, a female target audience empathizes with a male-gendered protagonist (or sets of characters) with feminine identity components. Since these female stand-ins are featured in narratives for female audiences, the plot or major force driving the plot is often romance, and so we have two (or more) male-bodied characters in a romantic situation. In Japan, this genre is established in print and television media as *yaoi*, but in the USA, *slash* is limited to fanworks (especially fan fiction), grassroots creative and interpretative reactions to male-dominated character-driven narratives.

Fascinatingly, yaoi and slash originated within a couple years of one another in Japan and the US. In the late 1970s, doujinshi mangaka parodied the contemporary boy's platonic love stories, spinning them into romantic and sexualized versions. Also in the late 1970s, female <u>Star Trek</u> fans began writing fanfic about the protagonists of their favorite starship. Stories would be about Kirk and Spock, abbreviated K&S if the relationship remained platonic, or Kirk slash Spock, abbreviated K/S if the relationship became romantic/sexual. This coined the term "slash" for the future generations of fan fiction writers to codify their works.

In Japan, yaoi has become a well-established genre, even becoming a major avenue for media exportation, reaching its most recent peak in international popularity in 2009-2010. There are thousands of yaoi titles, but I will review a couple here briefly. Yaoi follows formulaic character roles: the protagonist is almost exclusively the "uke", the "receiver" or bottom of the sexual pairing, and the main romantic interest is the "seme", or the "attacker" or the top of the sexual pairing. Ukes are drawn effeminately, with large eyes characteristic of female or prepubescent boy characters, and often have feminine personality attributes. In <u>Junjou Romantica</u>[1], Misaki (girl name for a

---

[1] The manga started in 2002 and is still being written at the time of this edition. The first two seasons of the anime were released in 2008 and saw huge popularity in the US as well as Japan. The third season is being released in 2015.

boy character) spends much of his screen time cooking, cleaning, or thinking about dates. In <u>Okane Ga Nai</u> (1999-present,) uke Ayase becomes a domestic partner for the seme Kanou in lieu of working a job. The roles these male (uke) characters play are traditionally facets of femininity.

Slash is harder to define as it remains a grassroots literary movement with, as of yet, no institutionally-backed artifacts[1]. Like yaoi, slash is most often slanted through the point of view of the more effeminate, "bottom" character. These slash protagonists retain parts of their feminine identity while still being able to succeed in their professional lives and hold equal footing with their romantic partners.

Yaoi has been popular the world over, and slash is on an exponential growth of popularity over the past four years, gaining legitimacy by leaps and bounds over the past ten months. These two similar genres are inspected in more detail in the next chapter.

In a country where a woman is shot and killed for talking back to a catcaller--in a country where a woman

---

[1] The possible exception to this is Cassandra Clare's <u>The Mortal Instruments: City of Bones</u> which is based on her Harry Potter/Draco Malfoy slash fan fiction. For publishing, Harry was changed to a girl and certain other elements of the plot, world, and characters were altered in order to avoid copyright issues. However, if you squint really hard, you can still see the similarities to the base fanfic.

has to carry around her college mattress in order to get a fair acknowledgement of her sexual assault claim--in a country where there has yet to be a female president, American women are overburdened with the realities of a world set against them. They burn to fulfill their aspirations. In the quiet of their private lives, they turn to art to assuage the hurts of daily micro-aggressions and larger structural oppressions. Even in fantasy, they cannot fathom nor imagine a realistic female character that would believably solve the problems of micro-sexism and macro-chauvinism and accomplish their own personal goals and have a well-balanced family life. Such a woman is unbelievable. Such a woman is unimaginable. So we turn to male characters, who wouldn't have to deal with the problems we face. By displacing elements of our feminine gender identity, we are able to more easily process other elements of it. When we engage in these narratives, we suspend the feminine gender building blocks of "unhealthy beauty ideals," "sexism in the workplace," and "the dangers of travelling alone." With these parts of our identity temporarily displaced, we can focus and process other elements of our lives and our feminine identities, like "sexual agency," "building healthy, equal, and sustainable romantic relationships," or "balancing professional ambition and personal life."

Yaoi and Slash: Grassroots Literary Reactions to Male-Dominated Narratives and Media

Lens: Walking through the business section of a major bookseller, the shelves are littered with books describing lessons to be gained from the pornography industry in the cyber age of internationalism for the business world. If our culture can utilize such an industry to learn lessons about the globalized business world, then it is a legitimate line of inquiry to learn about our culture via probing the genres of yaoi and slash.

Now that we have introduced yaoi and slash, let us look deeper into similarities and differences of these two.

What are the differences between yaoi and slash?

The most obvious difference lies in the preferred medium. Japan has thriving comic book culture, so yaoi is mostly in manga form, while there are also light novels, audio adaptations, and, for some more popular works, anime versions. In the US, slash exists in literary fiction form, but there are more and more slash artworks to be found on sites like Deviantart and Tumblr.

Secondly, as mentioned in the previous chapter, gender roles are more traditionally defined in yaoi than slash. In yaoi, we see the seme and uke having sacrosanct roles, particularly in the bedroom. In slash, roles are more fluid. The slash equivalent of an uke is more masculine, and often the couples "switch" roles in the professional world, the familial world, and the bedroom.

Thirdly, yaoi fans are demonized and ostracized in Japanese culture. This negativity is, arguably, internalized as yaoi fangirls refer to themselves as "fujoshi" (腐女子) or "rotten[1] women". Since slash has been mostly a grassroots movement, it has escaped being the target of large-scale demonization. However, much of the previous (1995-2005 or so) negativity towards fan fiction in general could be attributed to the large amount of slash within it and the misogynistic and homophobic reactions to those works. Until the past couple of years, writing fanfic was a dirty little secret of authors and fans alike, but with fandom as a whole gaining recognition and validation, fan fiction, too, is seeing major improvements in popular perception.

Finally, yaoi is on the decline worldwide and domestically in Japan, while slash is gaining steam in the US. Yaoi appears to no longer fashionable in Japan, perhaps due to social stigma or perhaps due to inflexibility of the genre. In the West, however, slash is only becoming more popular and more visible. 2014 saw two great tributes to fan's engagement with their favorite

---

[1] "Fu", the first character of this term, also means "decay."

mass media series. BBC's <u>Sherlock</u> (which has at least 70,000 fanworks dedicated to it on the fanfiction website Archive of our Own, 40,000 of which are slash at the time of drafting this chapter) wrote Sherlock fans and their fan fiction theories into the script for the first episode of season three. In November 2014, popular US American series <u>Supernatural</u> lovingly dedicated their 200th episode to fan fiction authors by having the plot of the episode revolve around a Supernatural fan playwright whose work attracts the deadly goddess Calliope. (Supernatural has at least 88,000 fanworks on AO3, 55,000 of which are slash.) Slash couples were mentioned in both series, and Supernatural even referred to the scripted romance as "BM", a play on "BL" or "Boys' Love" another Japanese term for slash[1].

Yaoi and Slash: Not as gay as you think?

One of the more fascinating commonalities between yaoi and slash is their distinctiveness from gay fiction. Yaoi is different from "bara", or gay narratives for a gay audience, just as slash, also known as gay romance, is different from gay fiction. The trick is in the target audience: whereas yaoi and slash are for

---

[1] To be technical, BL refers especially to shounen-ai, or love between two boys (under the age of 18). I use "yaoi" as an umbrella term for all male-male fictions (of Japanese origin), despite its denotation of romance between two adult men. The American term "slash" is non-specific to the ages of the primary couple.

(generally heterosexual) women, bara and gay fiction are for homosexuals (generally men.) This distinction is most stark in Japanese media: yaoi features effeminate protagonists, while bara's protagonists are more masculine and more evenly paired with their partners. Yaoi plots feature women's challenges, while bara stories consistently address issues pertinent to the homosexual community. In slash, the difference is more nuanced and sometimes the boundaries blur. US American gender roles are less traditional than Japanese, and more US American straight women are likely to empathize with gay issues than their Japanese counterparts. These factors drive a meshing of slash and gay fiction that is absent in Japan.

What do yaoi and slash offer us that traditional mainstream romantic media do not?

Yaoi and slash have become popular in the United States by both repairing the damage that traditional romance does to women and filling demographic and interest group gaps glazed over by media for mass distribution. By being relevant and inclusive, slash's popularity has grown profusely over the past decade.

To begin, we inspect the failures of romance in the United States. There are four main critiques of mass media that are addressed by slash/yaoi. First is the objectification of women. This is a common critique of all narratives bound to a general audience: female characters are endpoints to achieve, a damsel in distress in need of rescue, a prize won after defeating a nemesis, or, more "progressively," a helpful sidekick. These female characters are flat for a vast majority of examples, but even in hugely popular BBC Sherlock miniseries, Irene Adler, a developed female character who is intelligent, capable, and has sexual agency, still needs to be rescued by Mr. Holmes at the end of her plot arc.

The second failing lies in mainstream romance and female-oriented narratives. In "chick flicks" and television targeting women, the endpoint of romance is marriage. Once marriage is achieved, there is no depiction of day-to-day romance after the "honeymoon phase" is over. Yaoi and slash both address the more quotidian relationship struggles, by either not allowing the marriage to be legal (i.e. gay men can't get married so it can't be the focus of their story) or, in slash, by progressing the story past the "falling in love" phase, through marriage, to pregnancy and child-rearing narratives. In slash "m-preg," or masculine pregnancy, is a common phenomenon in fictions: there are over 10,000 works tagged as m-preg on AO3. In other stories, the men find themselves as single dads where the mother either died or relinquished rights to the children. In these stories, women audiences explore more realistic approximations of the romantic struggles instead of the rosy depictions propagated by mainstream media.

The third failure of mass media romance is the lack of sexual agency for the "receiver" or "bottom" of the sexual act. If first-wave feminism dealt with women's agency in the political sphere (suffrage), second-wave feminism in the public sphere (workplace rights, reproductive rights in regards to access to birth control and abortion), perhaps the final wave of feminism deals with the internalization of equality, bringing agency to women in the most private of spheres--the bedroom. Indeed, third-wave feminism does address this issue, as well as a myriad of other nuances of the application of equality to gender ideas. Yaoi and slash keep sexual agency simple and clean by the removal of the female partner. Men, no matter if they are tops or bottoms, have sexual agency, and therefore there is no shame in having sex. To be exact, in yaoi, there is shame in the act of sex, but that is channeled through the idea of *homosexual* sex being shameful. In this way the traditional, feminine coy reaction to the act of sex can be reaffirmed. In many yaoi and almost all slash, however, the male characters with whom the female audience empathizes do have sexual agency, and thus this medium empowers women to have full ownership of their bodies and sexual drive. (This idea is revisited in section about omegaverse).

Fourthly, yaoi and slash are inclusive to more fringe communities than mainstream romance. Yaoi and slash, by bypassing traditional feminine reticence towards sexual activity, are open to more untraditional expressions and explorations of sexual desire. Kink, fetish, and multiple partners (i.e. free love and polyamory) are elements not uncommon to both forms. Ai No Kusabi[1], one of the most popular and often noted as a "defining" yaoi story, uses bondage and slave-master role play as a layering power structure in its allegorical story about post-WWII political marginalization, urbanization, modernization, and the rift and unequal relation between the developed world and the countries still developing. As for slash, one needs only look at the most popular tags on AO3 to find what women are exploring in their fiction: about ten percent of the top 200 tags are directly related to untraditional sexuality. Listings such as "asphyxiation" and "BDSM" are juxtaposed among more banal tags like "cuddling and snuggling", and the surprisingly ordinary "weather".

What exactly is the relationship between yaoi and the homosexual demographic?

This is a common discussion point at cons. The starting point is the question of whether yaoi and slash

---

[1] This story was released as a light novel in the 1980s. It was made into an anime in the early 1990s then remade in 2012.

challenge heteronormality. Since yaoi's seme and uke are male and female stand-ins, I would argue that yaoi does not challenge heteronormality in Japan. Slash, with its more realistic relationships pairing two people of the same gender, does challenge heteronormality. Indeed, many slash realize *homonormality.* This leads us to the idea of the fetishization of homosexuality. Do yaoi and slash fetishize gayness? Absolutely. I would argue that, for the current global climate of contention around the GLBT population, gays being fetishized may not be a bad thing. It's easier to step down from a pedestal than it is to pull yourself out of a hole, fetishization is preferable to demonization, and at least, while being fetishized, one is still visible.

Only in regards to the US American audience do we venture to the realm of if slash is queer baiting. Queer baiting is a recently-coined term to describe the idea that creators of a pair of same-sex characters inject sexual tension into the scenes between those two characters in order to "bait" or attract a gay audience, only to never allow the sexual tension to be resolved into a relationship. Slash is very diverse in quality, content, and maturity level of the author. The best slash are generally written by highly intelligent, if not highly educated, women generally aged twenty-four to thirty-four who are concerned with producing good stories. These stories use the medium to explore the human condition, relationships, and the societal structures that affect these concepts.[1] They do not queer bait. More recently, another sizable portion of writers has emerged—middle school and high school students. This younger demographic is much more concerned with achieving a high number of readers or greater exposure of their work, and *may* use slash as a tool to garner greater attention to their work.

Will yaoi or slash become mainstream in the US?

For now, a conditional no. A slash (as Americanized yaoi) narrative would be most likely to succeed in indie film form, but the backlash from the gay community of it as "queer baiting" in addition to alienation from heteronormative, mainstream audiences would result in an unsuccessful box-office turnout.

Here is the condition: a form of slash could be successful, and has the ingredients to be a popular and impactful work of media. Omegaverse, heretofore undiscussed, is a subgenre of slash that is situated in the middle of gender ideas exposed in yaoi and slash. Omegaverse utilizes the addition of "designations" or "secondary genders" with the traditional male and female gender binary. It features six categorizations of people: alpha male, alpha female, beta male, beta female, omega male, and omega female. In this universe, one's

---

[1] Mostly white women in this age group have historically been the largest demographic of writers of fan fiction.

alpha, beta, or omega status supersedes that of binary gender. As this is a universe of grassroots and ever-mutating and decentralized creation (incorporating elements of Blondies and Mongrels from the Ai No Kusabi narrative and the Sentinels and Guides[1] from The Sentinel universe) characterization of each of these groups organically varies. Generally alphas are leaders, physically stronger, and aggressive; betas are *normal*, without distinction, and often seen as worker bees; omegas are physically weaker, often regulated or confined to the domestic sphere, and sometimes suffer heats.

Omegaverse is uniquely situated for mainstream success as it addresses multiple burning issues in society and resonates on several levels. First, it addresses women's issues using a (masculine) omegan mask. Consider the following dialogue between an Alpha father and his Omega son in the omegaverse, slash fiction, "The Way Things Were."

> "I'm not useless." John stepped forward, fists clenched impotently. "I'm one of the smartest students in my year. I'm the best player on the team. I've already won awards for it- for all of it, if you'd just bother finding out…I have

[1] Character types from Canadian television series The Sentinel, which ran in the 1990s and then was syndicated on the US channel Syfy. Created by Danny Bilson and Paul de Meo.

friends. A job. I work hard and I don't sneak around behind yours or mum's back. I'm going to go to uni and have a career and be successful… I'm not useless just because I'm an Omega." He shouted, chest heaving, blood pounding in his ears, shaking from the rush of adrenaline at finally being able to say some of what he'd always wanted to say to his father. He wanted his father to respect him. To at least acknowledge that he wasn't worthless. That he had potential- potential that seemingly everyone else could see but him.

"None of that…means…shit." His father replied coolly, taking another drink. "You're an Omega, John. You can't overcome your biology. You can try." He smirked. "You can pretend you're something else, something better, and play rugby. Go to uni. Have friends. But it's all nothing. Because in the end? You're an Omega. It's who you are. Programed into your goddamn biology…and the entire world knows you're just there to get fucked."[1]

[1] http://archiveofourown.org/works/2630762 The Way Things Were by starrysummernights accessed 12/5/2014

This dialogue describes chauvinism and rape culture experiences in a raw form, but the blow is softened by the cognitive distance created by using a male character. Structural misogyny, rape culture, the biological imperative ("A man has needs") are hot topics increasingly present in popular discourse. This naturally flows into popular art, as seen in rape attempt scene in film <u>Divergent</u> earlier this year and <u>The Hunger Games: Mockingjay</u>'s forced prostitution of a secondary character (the blow once again softened by using a male character).

Omegaverse also addresses the new issue of sex horror[1]. One of the myriad social changes that swept our society with the advent of the internet was the evolution in the method young people sought after sexual education. Children are exposed to (and their inquisitive minds expose themselves to) an enormous amount of straight-male-targeted pornography that disproportionately exemplifies the most debase and perverse desires of a minority with means. Girls who watch this form of pornography are taught that sex is painful, degrading, and cruel, and thus they develop a sense of sex horror. These depictions in pornography stand in direct opposition to the common consensus that sex is a good thing, and so these young women create

---

[1] After the term "body horror" used to describe a grotesque genre of horror in which there are visceral reactions to graphically-depicted destruction or degeneration of a human body or bodies.

omegaverse fiction to span the two extremes. In their stories, the main plot-trope involves an omega who falls into heat, a period of sexual necessity, and must have sex with an alpha, who in many cases has nightmarish bestial genitalia, and the story resolves with the sex being enjoyable rather than the imagined and anticipated painful experience. I am certainly not suggesting that a story using this trope of omegaverse would be popular, but rather that a more accessible rendering of omegaverse would be buoyed by these scarily-common (nearly-normalized) stories.

What example of omegaverse would be successful? A story with a heterosexual alpha-omega main pairing with a male homosexual (A/O, A/B, or B/B pairing) secondary couple would be accessible to a mainstream audience, especially if the plot involved in a political upset having to do with gender legislation. One could widen the scope and audience by incorporating generational gap challenges and the idea of a structurally persecuted minority. Since there would be a need for a large amount of world development and background explanation, the best media form would be a novel or indie film. Since the main point of this resonance is non-traditional gender ideas and redefining gender (after all, six designations are more descriptively accurate than two genders), the best timing of release of such a narrative would be July through August 2016, to coincide with the Democratic National Convention, a time when antifeminist talking heads will be at their most virulent in the lead up to Hillary Clinton's run for President in the 2016 elections. If the story were to feature a female alpha (leader) and a male omega (support), the second best time for the release would be after Hillary's potential failure to win the general election in November[1].

If this window of opportunity passes, then the next time for omegaverse to gain popularity would be in seven to ten years, when the next generation is pushing the limits of normality and rebelling against their parents (Gen Y) in the most shocking and possibly revolting manner possible. Besides its shock value, omegaverse also bears several other hallmarks that flag it as a possible "next big thing". It resonates with an already active and tightly-knit community. It addresses the needs of a wider audience and the problems of mainstream media. Most remarkably, it has been acting like many other cutting-edge franchises: omegaverse has been circling the periphery of the mainstream, being consistently present in all major fandoms (and thus building a commonality between a wide range of audiences), and it has been constantly present over the past ten years. **In short, it is persistent and pervasive**.

---

[1] My headcanon for this involves two filmings of the movie: one with a male omega and female alpha and then filmed again but with a male alpha and female omega leads. If Hillary wins, the male alpha/female omega would be released. If she loses, the female alpha and male omega version would be released.

Omegaverse certainly has the potential break into the mainstream and garner both widespread popularity and a core of devoted fans, but still requires a good writer, a better story, and the best marketing that can provided in order to be a trendsetting success.

Is yaoi a global phenomenon?

Yes, since yaoi addresses women's issues of conserving femininity while integrating more "modern" (read: masculine) roles of being in the workforce or being professionally ambitious, it has struck chords in other countries where women face these dilemmas. In France, feminist scholars have studied the issues of childbirth and professional life, culminating in and stemming from the burning issue of early child care. In Germany, women struggle with the idea of having to become a "Superfrau," balancing career with the traditional three K's of women's life (Kinder, Küche, und Kirche, or children, kitchen, and church). Yaoi narratives, alongside shoujo and josei stories that address these issues, have seen success in these countries. China also has an underground yaoi movement, but with the government all but forbidding homosexuality, it remains ostracized, to the point of thirty-two yaoi mangaka being arrested in 2011 for their work[1].[2] The widespread popularity of this medium stems from a common reaction to a global shift in women's gender roles and the struggle women face incorporating new "progressive" ideals with traditional values.

Additional Notes:
- A soundtrack for this chapter can be found here: http://8tracks.com/softpowerpunch-428/disappearing-women-yaoi-and-slash
- Genderbending and Gender swapping information can be found on page 123 in the Addendum: Discard Pile.

---

[1] Accessed March 16, 2014. http://fanhackers.transformativeworks.org/2013/03/meta-32-fic-writers-arrested-in-china-in-2011-and-we-missed-it/

[2] Twenty more were arrested in April 2014. With yaoi and slash's growing legitimacy and their communities growing more organized, this time the arrests were publicly exposed and denounced on many international news and journalism sites.

Cultural Collage

Are the Otaku Globalization's First Children?

Post-Geographic Third Culture Kids

"Go abroad." This is the advice given to thousands of US college students each year. Having study abroad or living experience in a foreign country is perceived to be a universal boon to one's resume. Living in a new culture is likewise perceived as a plus no matter what your field: study abroad--it's not just for liberal arts students anymore! The experience of living abroad can be harrowing or euphoric. It can be beneficial or weakening to one's studies. It can be the most rigorous academic work or the most like a vacation one could have as student. It can ignite passions and extinguish dreams. Any experience abroad, even a bad one, is seen as a positive by employers, academic institutions, and any social network. Why then, if the experience itself can be so detrimental, is it in such high regard and even higher demand?

Part of this is perception. Certainly, having an association with someone who comes from a global background makes the company seem more globally-minded. "International experience" is an easy sell in the ever-globalizing world where we live. In many circles, experience abroad is an exotic quality that purveys a certain type of affluence and connectivity that is essentially appealing.

For the quality of having experience abroad to become such a salient and interdisciplinary desired trait, more than appearances must keep it in high demand.

Experience in a foreign culture has not always been seen in such a positive light. During the 1950s-1970s, many dignitaries (and other personnel aiding in the execution of the Marshall Plan,) agreed that abroad experience was *damaging* to children's psyches and social development. American children born to parents living abroad were called "Third Culture Kids," a term to which I was first introduced in a wonderful Advent sermon at the American Church of Paris. Historically, Third Culture Kids (TCKs) were characterized as socially stunted, unable to connect with their national culture or the foreign culture in which they were immersed. They identified with neither the foreign culture where they lived nor the one printed on their passports, and thus became a part of a Third Culture, only able to truly identify with other TCKs. Furthermore, they were seen to withdraw from individuals of only one culture, unable to adapt to circumstances and perceptions of their mono-cultured peers.

From what I've seen and experienced, this alienation stems from sociolinguistic edifices internally erected during the abroad experience. Individuals (here: children) have exposure to certain ideas and linguistic codes to express those ideas in their primary culture[1]. At school or in the public sphere, they are given a different set of linguistic codes to express the foreign (secondary) culture's differing ideas. Certainly, discussing the disparity or conflict between these two codes is a strong point of mental deliberation as individuals navigate reconciliation of the two. The acts of resolving the two creates and substantiates a tertiary culture. This experience shapes personality and one's life and easily becomes a point of commonality and resonance among individuals who have experienced living in foreign cultures. The dwelling in the third culture was, I assume, seen as a negative force for self-alienation from secondary cultures during that time period. After enough time elapsed for these first generation, third culture children to stabilize and grow into adults, their capacity to utilize multiple advanced sociolinguistic codes emerged to be neither destructive nor wholly positive for overall communication.

As related later in the fourth Advent sermon, and more recently commonly discussed (thank you, internet), the popular opinion of expatriate families (as well as child psychologists' stance) of TCKs has completely flipped. Abroad experience is now perceived to be beneficial to a child's development, as TCKs are thought to have better communication skills than their mono-

---

[1] Primary culture for those born domestically is native land culture. Primary culture for those born abroad is culture practiced at home with their parents.

cultured peers, a greater capacity to empathize with those from different points of view and circumstances, an ability to adapt easily (they are often likened to chameleons), and are proven diplomats for mediating conflict and clashes of differing points of view. All these skills are sharpened from living immersed in a foreign culture.

For college-aged students, these arguments also apply, but they are supplemented with the added quality of grace under fire and the capability to easily handle stressful situations and crises.

What does this have to do with Japanese influence in the USA? **I posit that the Otaku of the Toonami Generation underwent a new form of <u>post-geographic acculturation</u>, resulting in the formation of a new type of third cultured children.**

When I first began interacting with Otaku at anime cons in 2012, the threads of dialogue were always similar. The main impetus for individuals to attend a con was the feeling of "community" and "being at home" with other Otaku. They could connect with other Otaku where they could not with individuals in their immediate communities. They felt alienated from their peers, who had not experienced this new and exciting Japanese culture as they had. They immersed themselves in the culture, absorbing the values, mores, and ideas transmitted through the media and any other supplemental research they may have pursued. They developed their own vernacular to describe their experiences and the tenets of Japanese culture which resonate most closely with their own personalities. These traits fit the same psychological profile of TCKs who grow up abroad. Otaku of the Toonami Generation have all the benefits and challenges of other children who are immersed in foreign cultures without ever leaving the borders of their homeland.

American Otaku are excellent global citizens. Having been exposed to foreign viewpoints in the media they consume, they are able to quickly understand different perspectives in their everyday life. Further along these lines, they are able to alter their own attitudes and outlooks and adapt quickly when circumstances demand change. From Japanese culture in particular, they have gained a deeper understanding of technology and its effect on our lives, empathy for differing personalities (especially those not represented in US mainstream media), patience for varying competence in self-expression and communication skills, and are teamwork gurus.

While getting to know Otakus on a personal level illuminates these positive qualities, nothing exemplifies the best traits of Otaku quite like the social institution of a Japanese culture convention. North America has thousands of anime cons. The top five, each of which is not for profit and volunteer-run, see an excess of twenty-five thousand attendees[1]. Most are multimillion dollar enterprises.

With all these advantages, Otaku bring great benefits to the companies and organizations to which they are dedicated. These advantages occur when an empowered American Otaku absorbs the best traits of Japanese culture, but what challenges lie for weaker individuals to be affected by the worst parts of that foreign culture?

Top Five Challenges to Otaku Culture:
1. Bullying of Adolescent Otaku
2. Body Shaming
3. Deletion of Racial Differences
4. Reinforcement of Anti-Social Behaviors and Social Withdrawal: NEETs, Boomerangs, and Shut-in Hikikomori
5. Misogyny and Madonna-Whore Complexes

Bullying of Adolescent Otaku
The first issue Otaku must face is that of bullying. During adolescence, it appears that a high proportion of Otaku are bullied both at school and at home via social media. According to one informal study[2],

---

[1]http://animecons.com/articles/article.shtml/1474/Ten_Largest_Nort h_American_Anime_Conventions_of_2013, Accessed Dec 14, 2014
[2] http://beneaththetangles.com/2012/11/19/anime-and-bullying-adolescent-

it is possible that half of all teenage Otakus have experienced bullying. Otaku are different from their peers in the area of socio-linguistic development. With language, one produces what one consumes, and Otakus' consumption of Japanese-based media alters their sociolinguistic pathways: even if they are reading subtitles or listening to a dubbed translation, exposure to different contexts and beats of conversation create a diversity and plurality in modes of expression.

Think of the lingual cortex as a dense forest. Ideas and language used to express them are pathways which one has forged through the trees and brush. (Those with more linguistic talent are armed with machetes for cutting through the creepers.) The more one walks these paths, the more one expresses these ideas, the quicker and easier the travel becomes. TCKs and Otaku foster pathways that their mono-cultured peers do not, so the pathways the peers take are more quickly navigated, and Otaku sometimes have to back off of one path to jump to another to be on the same page as their peers, resulting in a language delay. In some cases, the slower processing time to navigate between several paths is so impactful that some Otaku, much like their TCK peers, will default to a deferential personality type rather than struggle with awkward time gaps in dialogue. Certainly, this difference in socio-linguistic development (or, for sociologists out there--deficit in

otaku-dealing-with-bullies/ accessed September 14, 2014.

social capital) is not the only reason why a person may be targeted by a bully, but these circumstances do not help a temporarily trying situation.[1]

As Otaku mature, bullying becomes less of an issue, but the negativity remains. Adult Otaku face adversity from within and without: many have internalized the negativity they faced as a child and/or the social stigma they face as an adult. On the popular crowdsourcing definition site, UrbanDictionary.com, four of the top five definitions of "otaku" are negative. The most popular definition, with thousands of up-votes, characterizes Otaku as people who "don't have a life." This begs the question if other "fans" also don't have lives when celebrating their passion. It is a common argument in the nerd community: if sports fans aren't put down for spending hundreds of dollars and days of their lives enjoying and supporting their teams of choice, then why do we dismiss geeks for their hobbies or, in this case, Otaku for their enthusiasm of anime, videogames, or cosplay?

First of all, Otaku are once again disparaged for simply being outside of the norm. Secondly, and more specific to US American culture, is that we don't value play. In the early 1900s, German scholar Max Weber wrote a cogent treatise on the intersection of capitalism

---

[1] If you are bullied, talk to an adult who has your interests at heart, like a parent or a good guidance counselor, and understand that you are not responsible nor the cause of the bullying. Bullies bully. It's not the victim's fault.

and the Protestant faith. His analysis of our culture has become one of the top ten texts read by all US social scientists. He posits that, for cultures rooted in the Protestant faith, such as the USA, the idea of a "vocation" mitigates importance on work and being "occupied" by work. Our Protestant work ethic means we live our lives for our vocation, and hobbies are undervalued. Applied to the matter at hand, Otakus' time spent enjoying their passion is seen as "destructive" to their professional life.

Most Otaku of the Toonami Generation now are educated and have the knowledge and skillset to examine such negativity objectively and analytically, and the vocabulary both to express their experiences and to educate the younger generation on how to deal with adversity. Once again, anime cons prove to be examples of the best of Otaku culture, as many have had workshops and panels on combating Otaku stigma and overcoming bullying.

Deletion of Racial Differences

This is an issue for Otaku who consume visual Japanese popular media: manga, anime, and video games. Characters rendered in these media generally are highly stylized with pale, white skin, and hair colors ranging from flat black to red frizzy curls, from blonde spikes to knee length blue pigtails. The characters are not ethnically diverse because Japan isn't ethnically diverse.

According to the CIA Factbook, Japan's ethnicity breaks down into 98.5% Japanese, 0.5% Korean, 0.4% Chinese and 0.6% other. For comparison, in the US we have a population that is 80% white[1], 13% black, and 4% Asian. Americans who consume Japanese media become comfortable with a strictly white cast of characters. For whites, this results in increased blind privilege, inhibited socialization with minorities, and further estrangement from the other 20% of the US population. For blacks and other minorities, it is one more example of erasure and invisibility from global media.

The exclusion of people of color in the depiction of characters has varying impacts. As always, for those empowered, well-socialized, healthy Otaku, it can be non-issue. Many anime cons have ethnically diverse staffs, and minorities hold positions of power. For Otaku who are less healthy and feel disempowered, it is easy for the seemingly all-white casts to reinforce previously-held, negative racial stereotypes.

Body Shaming

Along these same lines is the depiction of normal weight in Japanese media. While 33% of adult Americans are obese[2], only 5% of Japanese are. The visual media of Japan reflects a healthier and thinner

---

[1] The Latino/Latina demographic is distributed among the black and white groups.

[2] BMI greater than 30, I assume.

populace. Among young American Otaku cosplayers, this means that many feel inadequate to emulate their favorite characters if they are not physically fit. At in-person events like cons, body shaming is publicly frowned upon. However, with the internet's mask of anonymity, weight-related insults, as well as racial slurs, are thrown about with abandon. Among more mature cosplayers, self-doubt evaporates as they accept their bodies, have healthier self-images, and understand completely that characters in anime/manga/videogames *do not have realistic proportions,* as part of Japanese style features super long legs and extremely large eyes. Fantastical expectations for one's body do not apply to a cosplayer who has a healthy mindset, but younger Otaku are targeted and impacted by ridiculous and needlessly demeaning comments.

Reinforcement of Anti-Social Behaviors

Culture shapes individuals to function in certain ways. Culture can also stimulate certain unhealthy individuals to dysfunction in other ways. Within the US, I have observed that Social Anxiety Disorder is most common in individuals from mid-Atlantic suburban culture, less common in New England culture, and rare in Southern culture. Others have recorded a stark difference in the amount of children diagnosed with ADHD in America versus France: 9% of the children from the land of red, white, and blue have been diagnosed with ADHD while for the land of the blue, white, and red has only 0.5%.[1] As a political scientist, I see these differences as indicative of a sort of macro-psychology, while psychologists may refer to it as country-based psychosocial influence.

When two cultures mix, the game changes. I believe that the layering of certain cultures upon one another can reinforce an individual's positive traits as well as exacerbate the negative ones. As the USA has a problem with children and young adults experiencing ADHD, Japan has a problem with young people experiencing acute social withdrawal, shutting themselves in and pulling away from all social and even familial contact. These individuals are called *hikikomori*, literally "pulling inward, being confined."[2] Inability to cope with the outside world is a gradient, and closer to healthy on that sliding scale are Japan's NEETs and Freeters. A NEET is a young person who cannot cope or cannot find employment and has given up trying to do so. They often stay at home with their parents or grandparents, and their livelihoods are provided by their families. They are "Not in Education, Employment, or Training." Similarly, a Freeter works only part time, still

---

[1] http://www.psychologytoday.com/blog/suffer-the-children/201203/why-french-kids-dont-have-adhd accessed December 15, 2014

[2] Teo, Alan. "Modern-Day Hermits: The Story Hikkomori in Japan and Beyond". Accessed June 14, 2014. https://www.youtube.com/watch?v=70bv5gaN4LI

depending on their families for a stipend to support the cost of living.

Japan's Freeters and NEETs parallel functionally and psychosocially with the Boomerang generation of the US: Boomerangs return home after a short stint away, usually in college, to continue to be supported by their family. According to the New York Times, nearly twenty percent of Americans aged 20-35 live with their parent(s)[1]. This occurrence in both cultures opened up avenues for Japanese media pertaining to adult financial dependence to be relevant and successful both domestic markets and abroad in the USA. The series Princess Jellyfish, an anime about a group of young women NEETs struggling with their underemployment, gender, and identity, saw a surge of popularity in the US in 2012-2013. Princess Jellyfish resonated with American Otaku who were facing similar struggles to the protagonists, or at least knew someone who was (a Boomerang). The series story gives voice and understanding to the difficult circumstances around young people today. Its positive influence *heals* a part of dysfunction found in both societies. At the same time, unhealthy individuals may view the story as a justification for their dysfunction, thinking, "See? They don't have full time jobs and are not self-sustainable. I don't have to be either."

---

[1] http://www.nytimes.com/2014/06/22/magazine/its-official-the-boomerang-kids-wont-leave.html?_r=0 accessed August 1, 2014

Other series do not *heal* individuals but rather reinforce the idea of social withdrawal and inability to function in society. In many stories, NEETs are not protagonists but secondary characters floating on the periphery. Any story with these characteristics holds potential to enable unhealthy behavior by passively accepting fiscally irresponsible habitude and anti-social actions.

Misogyny

If one lets Japanese media speak for itself, it appears that Japan's society leans more toward the binary, traditional idea of gender roles than America's does. In (Japanese) media designated for a general audience, female characters are relegated to being a prize or a nemesis. When they are integrated as members of a team of protagonists, their distinguishing characteristics are often purity, gentleness, and beauty. The population acts in accordance to such polarized perceptions of women by emulating role models put forth by media. Thus, one would expect the societal and economic role of women to remain more firmly tied to domesticity than ambition. The Economist published an article in May 2014 proclaiming, "Women's lowly status in the Japanese workplace has barely improved in decades, and the country suffers as a result." The article went on to include explanation of the term the "bamboo ceiling" that bars women from promotion to the top of corporations, after the American concept of a "glass ceiling." The bamboo ceiling, by comparison, is not nearly as transparent as the American equivalent, and much sturdier[1]. While the media portrayal of gender roles is not the singular factor in the shaping society and economy, it remains a salient contributor to the molding of such norms.

Japanese media's influence does not stop at the Pacific Ocean. We have seen many examples of the strong trade and importation of Japanese art and the ideas that come with it. For Americans, the transmission and edification of ultra-conservative[2] gender roles influences our culture in different ways. Once again, reaction to this influence is split between healthy and unhealthy individuals.

Some react in healthy ways. Otakus, especially adult women Otakus, emerge from the influx of varying ideas of societal and gender norms as strong, assertive, self-assured individuals. I see similarities between women in the Otaku community and women in STEM[3] careers: they are so well-acquainted with sexism and boy's clubs mentalities that their confident personalities are forged into a no-nonsense, straight forward manner,

---

[1] http://www.economist.com/news/briefing/21599763-womens-lowly-status-japanese-workplace-has-barely-improved-decades-and-country accessed July 28, 2014

[2] by American standards

[3] Acronym referring to the fields of Sciences, Technology, Engineering, and Mathematics.

tempered with ferocity, to boldly face all challenges, whether they be gender-specific or not. On the other hand, less strong women in both communities conform and defer to the normal gender roles and biases, sinking into the background with more demure temperament rather than rocking the boat.

If one follows the idea that the mixing and superimposing one culture onto another can influence the macro-psychology of a population, we end in the very alarming of concept of two distinct cultures that disempower women in different ways merging to transmit very destructive ideas on a group of consumers. Extending this idea to the extreme, the combination of two nuanced rape cultures influencing a population can possibly have dangerous results.

Rape is an issue in both cultures, and is increasingly incorporated into narratives in both Japanese and American media. Shoujo has used rape scenes in character development so often that it has become a trope. Hana Yori Dango has at least five attempted rapes, and even the positively viewed Ouran High School Host Club features an episode revolving around the necessity for the female protagonist to not "ask for" being raped by engaging boy bullies. As for American major motion pictures, we recently saw our first on-screen rape attempt in which a girl protagonist was pinned down and straddled by a man who held a position of power over her in the film Divergent.[1] Using such scenes is a double-edged sword: some will walk away feeling less alone in the knowledge that there are other rape survivors, and others will believe the idea of raping someone is *normal*.

More often we see examples of less violent aggression against women. As the roles women play in media are flattened to a binary, so is the consumer's expectation of women in real life, consciously or subconsciously. The objectification of women has been a problem for both countries at least since post-World War II. In Japan, there is the perception that many salary men seek out paid companions to appease sexual appetites that their honorable wives do not fill. In America, we have the term "Madonna-whore complex" to describe a person who sees women as either pure and wholesome or sexual and debase. This psychological complex is often cited as the reason why serial rapists commit their crimes.

As two cultures that are oppressive of women converge on a population, we may expect to see individuals with very strong, toxically unhealthy ideas of gender norms. With two different cultures presenting varied, nuanced explanations for the objectification, infantilization, and sexualization of women, an unhealthy individual could be socialized to be destructive force.

---

[1] Yes, this was a nightmare of the protagonist Tris; however, real or not real, watching the scene has the same effect on viewer's psyche.

The story does not end here. In the Otaku community, we have seen women, especially female cosplayers, fight back against unwanted masculine attention and objectifying behavior at cons. "Cosplay is not Consent" is the slogan for a recent campaign of young women to gain recognition and respect from their fellow community members after fighting an increasing amount of privacy invasions, micro-aggressions, and personal assaults while wearing costumes of their favorite characters.

Chapter Conclusion:

Politicians worldwide accept the power of media and artists. If one doesn't respect them, one won't remain a politician for long. There's a reason why journalists and artists are the first to be imprisoned or killed when a dictator takes over. Artists themselves tend to be wholly (blissfully) ignorant of the power they wield. Some are shocked into contemplating their effect on people's psyches, a burden author J.D. Salinger grappled with after several murderers sited his fiction as impetus for their assassinations. From what I've seen and experienced, all artistic creators face a dilemma: with each world or narrative you create, you either reinforce dominant paradigms or subvert them. If you write about a society free from racial differences, there will probably still be heteronormality. If you create a story with nontraditional gender roles, you may ignore class.[1] Higher up the food chain, major publishing houses and film production companies pick and choose which "progressive" elements to incorporate in each product, for taking all of them creates a story too slow in plot development or too much suspension of disbelief that it will no longer resonate with audiences. Art is powerful. It teaches us much about ourselves and molds our children. It can be the greatest unifier and the most destructive poison for our world.

---

[1] Yaoi and slash often take place in "Cinderella" settings where the characters are rich without having to work.

What Makes Transnational Media Tick?
An Introduction

What makes some art transport profitably overseas and others not? This was the subject of a thesis I wrote while studying at Université Paris VII Diderot: I used comparative analysis to create a list of commonalities of Edith Piaf and Daft Punk as model artists who gained popularity both within France and the USA. These similar characteristics between the two musical phenomena yielded a type of profile criteria for a musical artist to be successful domestically and abroad. Qualities that hallmarked transnational success included being influenced by diverse artists outside of their immediate artistic and cultural sphere, maintaining creative rights, ability to connect and maintain relationship with audiences[1], and continuous transformative creativity while maintaining recognizable fundamental identity. I posited that meeting these criteria would bolster the chance of success in both countries.[2]

---

[1] Key elements of securing the target audience included well-orchestrated introduction as well as marketing to the target audience. It is also important to note that having an accessible format, in these cases song lyrics in English, was likewise essential.

[2] Since my production of that paper, the French artist Camille tried to crossover the Atlantic; however, without a proper marketing and introduction to the American audience, the effort failed. She also lacked the cultural resonance that both Edith Piaf and Daft Punk had tapped.

These qualities were in regards to particularly music and specifically France, but when dealing with the dissection transnational media, larger forces are at play. Japan and America already have a close, strong friendship with a stronger trade relationship between the two. Our positive relations are so strong, even other countries have taken note. Danish-produced webcomic Scandinavia and the World published a one-cell rendition of this mutual love in 2012 entitled "Fangirls." SatW features the misadventures of varying characters who are anthropomorphized nations. In this edition of the comic, a female Japan and a female America, each toting artifacts and accessories of the other's culture, exclaim, "Oh my god!!! I'm your biggest fan!!!"[1]

Our love of Japan is so strong it is frequently manifested in our popular culture. Outside of the internment awareness campaign of George Takei, elements of Japanese pop culture are often cultivated, integrated, or alluded to in our film and television media. In this year's (2014) Hannibal, a highly critically-acclaimed NBC miniseries featuring Hannibal Lecter and characters from Thomas Harris's The Red Dragon, the second season is completely structured after traditional Japanese Kaiseki dinner, with episodes named after course dishes, including Sakizuke, Naka-choko, and Mizumono. American viewers are now aware and

---

[1] http://satwcomic.com/fangirls accessed August 14, 2014

curious about this element of Japanese cuisine. Shortly after the season's premiere, Kaiseki dinners were in high demand, resulting in many societies for the promotion of Japanese culture and other groups affiliated with Japan to feature them during fundraising banquets.

Another American television series to integrate Japanese culture is the ten-year running Supernatural. It has featured several "monsters" based on Japanese folklore, including buruburu and okami. Additionally, it has referenced Japanese films like Godzilla vs Mothra and Battle Royale, as well as the recurring mention of hentai[1] by bad-boy protagonist Dean. This spring (2014,) MTV's Teen Wolf featured a Japanese centric season (3B,) which employed elements of Japanese mythical yōkai creatures, kitsune (fox spirits) and oni (demons)

Beyond television, American film elevates Japanese culture in increasing frequency by paying homage to Japan's style and imagination. Pacific Rim (2013) and the Transformers film series (2007-2014) both borrow heavily if not directly from Japanese media. These homegrown pastiches and tributes[2] to Japan edify and proliferate its "cool" public image[3].

Looking back at Japan's exportation of media to America, we can break down successful works and

---

[1] Japanese anime of sexual nature.
[2] Hunger Games pun intended. The American series is often likened to the Japan's Battle Royale.
[3] "Cool Japan" is both a Japanese government-sponsored PR initiative and a television program on NHK.

franchises, taking them apart and seeing what makes them tick for the two peoples.

In high school English, my blessed teacher Dr. JT stressed literary criticism by inspecting the theme and technique of works. Starting with this simple method, the analysis of transnational media lies along these same lines: we must look at the content and casing to discern transnational merit of works.

When analyzing the broad spectrum of all media, content and casing remain rather nebulous concepts. Casing refers to the techniques used in the execution of a piece of art, while content refers to the underpinning theory or underlying theme it communicates. Another way of looking at this duality is that casing is the packaging or production (value)[1] of a work, while its content is the message or moral portrayed.[2] Casings envelop content: in Great Art, they conduct meaning, while in lesser works they act as distraction from it, creating dissonance in the cohesion of the work, detracting from the quality of the end product.

Content and casing are of equal import, but both are to be employed concisely and with economy. During

---

[1] For visual media, casings are often the "hook" for audiences. What a film looks like is presented in the trailer, including snippets of the highest cost scenes.
[2] Specifically when dealing with short stories, casing could refer to the world, genre, and plot, while content would be manifested in the story.

the creation and conceptualization phase, if too much emphasis is placed on casing, the final product is formulaic and empty. Case in point: <u>Superman: Man of Steel</u> (2013) which has astronomical production value but no well-developed content. On the other end of the spectrum, any work that is all content with very attention to casing or execution would be inaccessible and unmarketable to a large audience. Examples of such works remain obscure and are mostly found as crowd-published literary pieces penned by an author who lives in his own head, or video games designed by someone who only cares about their own enjoyment and not the player's, or pretentious YouTube video projects with double digit hit counts.

Casings are analyzed on an *accessibility* gradient ranging from overused cliché or trope, through the familiar, then to novel[1]. Genres, structures, styles, and techniques[2] used within a work are more accessible the more familiar they are, and are harder to process if they are newer and unfamiliar. If one were to assign

---

[1] One day, I'd like to explore deeper into the concept of "weirdness" and how various populations embrace or reject it. Japan certainly embraces weird things almost to an extreme; France, especially French fashion, esteems weird trends; I'm currently too close to and deep in American culture to discern how we react to weirdness.

[2] Visuals and auditory layers as well. Do the characters look like me? Do they sound like me? Is the music familiar? Are the diegetic and non-diegetic sounds familiar and easily understandable? What plot devices and types of characters are employed? Certain casings are more accessible to certain socio-economic groups and cultures (i.e. in the US, poorer populations historically do not respond well to sci-fi.)

numerical value along this spectrum, we would see that younger people on average respond more favorably to material found on the novel side of the scale, as opposed to perhaps the elderly demographic, who would respond more strongly to more familiar casings and styles of execution, closer to the overused, tropic area.

Contents are analyzed on what I have seen as *resonance*. Law and Order creator Rene Balcer also described this idea as "cultural pressure points.[1]" For franchises and larger works of art, people want something they can sink their hearts into. One feels resonance when one empathizes strongly with a character, or a certain story touches one's heart, or one experiences catharsis after watching a protagonist (or antagonist) struggle. Great Art is often qualified by the elicitation of this type of emotional response. Resonance points, then, are traced from historical, political, economic and sociocultural events through population's experiencing these episodes to nuggets of truth that deal with, comfort through, or explain these matters. Points of resonance echo in the heart of a people.

All this muddled theory makes more sense when applied to actual works. Let's develop this further looking at two examples of popular American media previously introduced.

---

[1] In a talk at University of Pennsylvania's Kelly Writer's House, October 30th, 2014.

Teen Wolf is housed in a high school genre, using the familiar young adult structure of absent parents and inept teachers. It also utilizes familiar folklore, specifically werewolves and, later, other fantastic anthropomorphic creatures. Its presentation of scenes both real and unreal blurs the lines of fantasy and reality, a common cinematographic ploy. All of these elements yield a familiar while not too-cliché casing. The content of this series touches on several resonance points: In the story, the protagonist is bitten and turned into a werewolf without his consent, and his ability to exert self-control and even self-awareness is brought into question. This resonates with burning issue of consent in our society and popular discourse. The friendship and bonding of individuals who are very different in personality, temper, and background (read: species) presented in the story resonate with our society in two ways: in a historical sphere, US society is founded on the idea of integrating and embracing diversity (i.e. the inclusion of differing individuals) and, more personally and immediately relevant to current audiences, the increasing visibility and importance of found families[1] plays a salient role in many Americans' lives. With the inclusion of several well-developed female characters, women's agency

---

[1] A "found family" is based on relationships and social ties rather than the blood ties of a traditional, biological family. As US Americans become increasingly mobile--Last time I checked, the average American moved once every eight to ten years--found families become more important with new locales.

94

resonates in the story as well. Family rounds out the final resonance point, as the role of family plays in the process of growing up is a recurring theme throughout the seasons.

Supernatural operates within some of the same casings: absent or flawed adult role models, folklore becoming real, and the lines of truth and perception are blurred. Additionally, this show cashes in on brotherhood and the recent popularity of "bromance". The content corresponds to these structures: morality is a large theme inspected as the male protagonists mature, cycle from reactive to proactive characters, and change their perspective from a black and white idea of good and evil to include more shades of gray. Second to morality, another resonance point tapped is the struggle of balancing familial responsibilities with professional ambition. Using gender identity displacement, the pressure to reconcile antithetical traditional with progressive roles is presented especially in season five. The (male) protagonists are confronted by ancient and almost absolutely powerful adversaries, who compel Sam and Dean into proscribed, traditional paths, outright telling them at one point--in a brilliant ripping from Fox News talking heads--to "know your role." This application of the burning issue of changing gender roles (especially in regards to women's roles) is a point of resonance for many women from differing countries, making the show relevant to their lives and exportable across borders.

The most salient works of Great Art marry casing with content. This is difficult when imagining a single audience, but grows trickier when the ingredient of internationalism is included. Internationally popular casings are fleeting and transient, and symbolism varies greatly (in variety and significance) from the East to the West. A look and feel (casing) of a work may be novel one place and overused somewhere else. Content similarly differs, yet we can investigate and examine pervasive and extensive resonance points that tap into people's emotions across borders.

Tracing Trends of Transnational Resonance

Resonance can be discerned by demographic, thematic, social movement, and crisis issue subjects. In order to limit the realm of possible resonant points, let us first investigate what type of resonant points will *not* succeed transnationally. Then we will ease our way into veins that have and may in the future translate across borders: starting with shared generational experience, we will then explore five topical burning global issues that hold potential to stimulate transnational resonance in narratives.

Null Hypothesis: What will resonate in only one culture?

Narratives that reflect or are reactionary to political, social, or economic events bounded geographic, states' borders will not resonate across those borders. In other words, a story focused on a historical event that effect only the lives within one country will resonate well in that country, but not in others who do not share that connection of experience. This idea seems simple, but many of the most successful stories do not label themselves as integrating the causal event. One must analyze the work to find the deeper subtexts that are at play. Extremely Loud and Incredibly Close is obvious in its tapping into 9/11 trauma, but Star Trek

Into Darkness does not as openly nor directly build on post-9/11 experience, yet draws resonance from popular understanding of that period. In this same vein, the Japanese anime feature Wolf Children was largely successful in domestic markets, but, as the resonance point was the trauma from the 2011 tsunami, the vast majority of Americans would not and have not responded as deeply to this story and its characters. Subtext can be as important as context when determining possibility of transnational resonance.

Tracing Generational Resonance in the United States

"Every epoch dreams its successor" -Jules Michelet

Over the last year, I have seen the rise of a new generation of Americans. In analyzing and distinguishing US American generations by resonance points, I have sketched the following framework for characterizing generations and their interests.

Generation - Approximate Birth Year (current age) - Defining Historical Events - Generational Response - (Fought for Civil Rights and Improved Life circumstances of) Minority or Disadvantaged Group in the Public Eye

Generation X - 1963-1983 (31 - 51) - born after the Baby Boom, coming of age during the Cold War - highest rate of volunteerism among the active generations, are currently "set in their ways" and no longer embrace large changes - Struggled for the integration of Civil Rights into everyday life and improved circumstances of Racial Minorities, especially African Americans

Gen Y - 1984-1989 (25-30) - last generation to remember a time before the internet - grapples with change, but embraces it; adapts to use swiftly-changing technology - (Minority in the public eye) homosexuals

Millennials - 1990-1997 (17-24) - first generation born into the digital age (i.e. after internet and cellphone became consumer electronics;) their childhood is defined by the great hope that internet would change the world for the better; grew up with the expectation of instant gratification due to the internet changing society -- Disillusionment and inability to grapple with change after an adolescence that occurred at the same time as large societal restructuring (effects of the internet, 9/11.) This disillusionment is manifested in the rise and popularity of emo-music and the popularity of narratives with darker tones. Overwhelmed by the plurality of ideals and identities presented to them, Millennials are characterized to have a lack of curiosity. (They have a "no news is good news" mentality.) – Public eye focused on ableism, but also on same groups as previous generations.

Hacker Gen - 1998-2003 (11-16) - The younger siblings of Millennials and exposed to their darker YA narratives, these young people see the world as filled with systemic flaws and strive to fix or circumvent them[1]. Reactionary to Millennial despair and breakneck speed[2]. - Adept to change and curious in nature. - Minority in public eye-TBD, probably redefinition of gender roles and transgendered people.

Generational resonance is problematic due to its direct relation with the age of the population. People are not only affected by the events of their time, but by the life events occurring (going to school, marriage, employment, retirement, etc.) Adding generational resonance as a layer to any narrative is powerful, but with transnational resonance one would have to keep in

---

[1] The idea of hacking is certainly pervasive in today's American culture. There's a "life hacks" TED talk playlist, and one can easily find "job hack" advice on websites. This young generation grows up aware of all the permutations of this idea, but also are exposed to popular narratives in film and television that idolize hackers, their mentality, and their abilities.
[2] One of the fad terms developed in the Hacker Gen subculture is "slow your roll." In direct opposition to the need for instant gratification and instant achievement in the Millennial generation, "slow your roll" means to slow down and re-evaluate where you are going and what you are doing in view of the larger picture. A boy who asks his girlfriend to marry him after their second date may be told by the girl to "slow your roll." It can also mean "Don't count your chickens before they hatch": a student who is bragging about the changes he will put into place as team captain before tryouts could also be told by a friend to "slow your roll."

mind that events that stimulate resonance in one country may not ping on the radar of a population of another country. That being said, as globalization plays an increasing role in the lives of citizens around the world, one may expect there to be more common events and experiences from which to draw resonance.

In this conversation of trans-Pacific resonance, we can cross reference the sketch of generational resonance in the USA to Japanese target demographics of narratives. One previously untapped, shared generational resonance of Japan and the USA is their aging populations and its effect on the younger generations. Twenty-five percent of Japanese are over 65, while a similar percentage of Americans are over the age of 55[1]. Certainly there have been Japanese narratives engaging the intergenerational struggle between young and elderly, but none have come to mainstream America. In the USA, we have had several films that incorporate aging GI generation and/or Baby Boomers as protagonists, often with younger generations among the supporting characters: 2010's RED and its 2013 sequel, 2012's Robot and Frank, and 2013's August Osage County. A Japanese anime, especially if in Studio Ghibli form (read: casing), could tap into this trend and find widespread success in both countries. A live action film could also succeed, but would be limited to the small,

---

[1] CIA Factbook

independent audience that enjoys foreign films with subtitles. Add in generational struggle of gender roles, and one may have a viable description of a possible narrative and character listing for a piece that would resonate in both countries: speculatively, aging grandfather struggles with adapting to new technology and connecting with his twenty- or thirty-something granddaughter.

Another example of trans-Pacific generational resonance lies in the previously mentioned phenomenon of the NEET/Boomerang parallel. This generation is responding to similar events--shifting of employment expectations from holding one job one's entire life and the global recession of 2008-2009---in a similar manner on both sides of the Pacific. One may predict that NEETs and Boomerangs may transition out of their dependent lifestyle in a similar manner. (That is, where are the characters from Princess Jellyfish ten years later?) This would create an opportunity for a new resonance point between the two countries at that time.

As for the Hacker Gen, Korean media shows the most promise for capturing that demographic. On the playing field of countries who export their culture, South Korea holds the largest proportion of 20-somethings. When the Hacker Gen reaches its post-college disillusionment, a narrative from Korea incorporating the difficulties of being single and in the transitional stage of professional and personal life would be the most advantageous to succeed in both cultures. Another element to integrate into this story could possibly be the idea of "skin hunger," whereas many of the Hacker Gen were aware or involved in the "Free Hugs" movement. This element could be too novel to integrate, but if another similar social movement like the Free Huggers comes into fashion, then skin hunger as part of the single 20-something life experience could be an essential point of resonance. There is already an Asian near-equivalent to utilize: "skinship".

Now that we've explored what will *not* resonate across borders, and generational resonance common between *two* countries, let's further widen the view further global issues.

Five Global Issues to Trace Transnational Resonance

1. There is a global challenge to traditional women's gender roles. With countries' economies impacted by mounting pressure to stay competitive on a global market, every state feels the necessity for women to join the workforce and attain a higher education in order to succeed in their jobs. We have already discussed how yaoi and josei narratives that build upon this resonance point have garnered relevance in other countries. This resonance point is also one of the main propelling force behind the international success of many the United

States' female-centric narratives popular since the 1960s, but most recent and powerful example of this would be <u>The Twilight Saga</u>.

2. The impact of technology and the digital age is another global issue that finds similar reactions in various countries' media. Dialogues vary greatly as technology plays an extensive and nuanced role in individuals' lives. Narratives will vary in relevance with news developments: if there is political struggle of net neutrality, one would expect stories addressing who owns and controls technology to be popular; if there is a scientific study about the effect of screen time on social development, then one would expect a story about moderation or transition of communication modes to be of interest. If a high priority or large scale hack is in the news, then information security would be a relevant theme. The trick lies in the diverse ways technology is distributed and acted upon in various states. For example, until recently, Japan and the US lead per capita screen time consumption over European countries by a sizable margin, and thus there was a similar gap in the role and manner in which technology influenced everyday life for citizens in those states. Art integrating or responding to screen time and technological fluency then would

resonate with Japanese and US audiences but alienate their European counterparts.

3. In the fallout of the global climate crisis and greenhouse gas awareness, the environment remains another tempting point of resonance as the issue is both pervasive and dramatic, but it is a problematic resonance point to engage. Environmental concerns are tightly tied to natural resources and geography of the state in question. While Japan may be concerned about deforestation, America is more concerned about smog and fossil fuels depletion. While many Americans understand the environmental commentary in Studio Ghibli's <u>Ponyo</u>, it is not as relevant to them as it is to Japanese audiences. It is also important to remember that environmental concerns are only relevant to affluent audiences as those who are living hand-to-mouth tend to not highly prioritize austerity measures.

4. Urbanization was a fad resonance point in the 1990s and early 2000s, but may see a swing back into popularity in the coming years. In 2001 <u>Metropolis</u> capitalized on this resonance with a beautifully crafted anime feature film that enjoyed moderate success in France and the US. South African film <u>Totsi</u> also integrated a commentary on the unsustainability of high-speed urbanization in 2005, and has been

garnered respect in indie audiences in the United States since its release. As culturally-specific architecture and city planning are inextricably related to the building of cities, this resonance point would be most effective in a science fiction or fantasy setting, where the world would be completely novel to all audiences.

5. For lack of a better term, the final subject heading is "globalization" itself. Like technology, this resonance point is to be examined in the context of smaller issues and across contexts. Globalization has differing influence on various generations, and could possibly exacerbate generation gaps in various countries simultaneously. On a larger scale, do certain countries acting as cultural hegemons threaten the autonomy and native cultures of other states? The answer to this question garners critical importance when tensions between states rise. Media and narratives that take one side or the other of this debate quickly become grassroots propaganda for or against the state and its policy.

We have now traced the drive of transnational media, from media that resonates *intra*nationally, internationally, and globally. Resonance analysis lies in the subtext and comprehensive understanding of both a target audience and the creators of the artwork. It is certainly easier to capitalize on trends in the casing of transnational media, rather than the content, as trends in casings are highly visible and quantitative, while trends in resonance are intuitive and qualitative. However, the marriage of these two yields the most accurate examination of art as possible successful transnational franchises.

Additional Note:

- In the Addendum: Discard Pile is a note on the shared resonance of "Epicness" between Japan and the US on p. 122. Please note that all articles in the Discard Pile are unedited and un-betaed.

Tips on Crafting Transnational Media

Having explored and identified qualities that drive transnational media, especially narrative media, we may now speculate how to create and ensure future international success via reverse engineering an artwork.

Step One: Work with artistic team to create a work with high-quality casing and content. Teams, having a diverse background and experience pool, are more flexible with the creation of an artwork than individuals who have a singular vision and voice over the project. Certain types of artists are preferable to advise (read: instruct) than others. In an interview about writing the soundtracks for the popular videogame series Final Fantasy, composer Nobuo Uematsu contrasted his organic creative process with other composers, explaining that he would ruminate on a certain theme or melody and then build from that, while other would create chord progressions and sound structures and then fill in the gaps.[1] In my experience with composers, cinematographers, and choreographers, I have noticed the division between those who favor creation by technique versus creation by organic inspiration and message. US author George R. R. Martin summed this idea up quite elegantly when he explained, "I think there

---

[1] Distant Worlds: Music from Final Fantasy Returning Home DVD from Square Enix and AWR Records, 2011.

are two types of writers, the architects and the gardeners. The architects plan everything ahead of time...The gardeners dig a hole, drop in a seed, and water it...they find out [what it is] as it grows." Process-oriented creators are more easily influenced at the developmental stage of a project, while organic creators will be more likely to guard their creative work. I also wonder if certain types of societies favor one type of creator over another: for example, if states which value the technical fields would produce more process-oriented creators, while states with a more service-oriented economy would produce more organic-method artists.

Or:

Step One: Select a work that will be successful domestically and in the target export country. Will it resonate with audiences in both places? Is it accessible to audiences of both places? The latter question is dependent on the casing's appeal to the audiences and is evaluated by investigating not only the relative production value of the work but also familiarity to the structures and techniques employed (i.e. do they facilitate ease of understanding and grasping the content?). While Baudelaire was correct in his statement that "Strangeness is a necessary ingredient in beauty," works that are too dissimilar from the norm will confuse and alienate audiences.

Step Two: Utilize local structures and institutions to win consumers. The first part of this is to re-evaluate the artwork in the eyes of the target audience. For art heading to foreign lands, sociolinguists or linguistic sociologists are **key.** A good sociolinguist will not only understand the ever-evolving mindset and desires of local target audiences but also be helpful in providing the most effective language to marketers who are crafting promotional material and translators who strive for the final product to be attractive and relevant to target consumers.

The second part is pure promotion. Different media are disseminated through different forms of marketing; however, when inspecting Japanese to US media, one main venue of marketing has been untapped: fan fiction. While Japanese markets have benefited for years from doujinshi work, US companies and creators are only very recently been aware of the marketing power of grassroots fanwork. Fanfic specifically eases the flow and acceptance of foreign media into the American market as *American consumer fan fiction writers adapt it to be more relevant to their lives.* Two years ago, Amazon opened the Kindle Worlds online e-publishing platform for fanfic writers to post and sell their stories. Companies that hold the licenses to Japanese media here in the US would only benefit from selling the part of the license that would allow American consumers to sell their fan fictions on Amazon. While the larger videogame companies that hold the rights to JRPGs like Final Fantasy and Kingdom Hearts would see largest gains in sales, distribution, and free marketing, smaller companies that hold the rights to anime and manga franchises could also see a bump in sales of their works. Fan fiction is the latest, untapped iteration of guerilla marketing and holds great possibility for companies vested in transnational media[1].

The third step is signal boosting via communities. This includes online community building through social media and the aforementioned fan fiction method, but face-to-face community building is also key. For Japanese media here in the US, this would be through presentations at anime cons, which Japanese and American companies already utilize effectively.

In conclusion, crafting transnational media does follow a type of procedure. Checking off items from this recommendation list may facilitate and ease the transition of media from one country to the next. However, it is important to remember that the world is always changing, and the modes and technologies which surface and are integrated into media forms are ever evolving. Understanding transnational media on the international scale is much similar to understanding it on the local scale: one must balance familiarity with

---

[1] See previous reference of the text-based, nonprofit Archive of Our Own fan fiction website securing over $100,000 in volunteer donations over only seven days in fall 2014 via a banner-based fundraiser.

technologies and techniques with the relevance of messages and meanings.

Timeline: Telegraphing Transnational Resonance

This is a composite of predictions from throughout the book, with a few extra thrown in for fun.

February 2015- As <u>Fifty Shades of Grey</u> hits theaters on Valentine's Day, the middle of the month is a prime time to market yaoi and other anime of a sexual or fetishistic nature. A "Fifty Shades of Hentai" or list of a similar nature would capitalize on the increased visibility and interest in this genre of anime/manga.

August 2015- This year marks the tenth anniversary of Hurricanes Katrina and Rita devastating the Gulf Coast. The hurricane victims will once again be in the news, and this would serve as an excellent time for a bi-national cooperative art project between hurricane and tsunami survivors. Such an initiative would also be of interest to the press as stories combining public interest, internationalism, and emotion would be lucrative to cover.

2015-2020 – As the last of the survivors of World War II die over the next five years, the general populace of both the US and Japan will be intermittently interested in "preserving the past"; our cultures, so immersed in fast-paced lifestyles and obsessions with novelty, will seek a balance by attempting to establish a sense of constancy by anchoring in the Past. Art that reflects nostalgia and remembrance of that period of time will continue to be popular on both sides of the Atlantic. By 2018, the US American market will be primed for another major narrative (film or book) tapping into this reminiscence trend. This interest will cease to be of major relevance to the younger generations once their living connection to the past has died.

2015-2025- Over the next decade, the evolution of gender norms will be another common resonance in the two societies. In Japan, intergenerational struggle between the elderly and their grandchildren will *possibly* serve as the main point of contention of intra-gender strife. In the USA, the struggle between Boomers, who lived during the Women's Lib movement and fought for their equality, and Gen Ys, Millennials, and Hacker Gen youth will continue to grow as the younger generations continually push for gender redefinition.

2015-20xx – Now and into the future, changing norms of permanency and ideas of stability will remain a common resonance between Japanese and US Americans. Older generations found necessary stability in external forms: employment, place of residence, long-term friendships, and living close to family. This is direct opposition to the truth of experience for younger generations who must build up permanency and stability in more internal sources, as individuals no longer have the same job or place of residence for their entire life, found family has thus become more important among the increasingly transient and fluid populations, and expressions of friendship are expressed through digital as well as physical means. The upset of stability certainly had deleterious financial effects for Japanese Freeters and US American Boomerangs, but younger generations hold promise of being able to successfully (and happily) navigate through such turbulent times. This idea of impermanent permanency, or "the only thing constant is change," will continue to be of relevance for both societies until globalization and technological evolution slows. Conservatism has had small push backs against such a wide-sweeping change, and we can expect to see a larger swing back to the "traditional" ideas of stability in the coming years, but such a large countermovement would need to be precipitated by a large, catalyzing event.

Late Summer, Early Fall 2016- Best time for an adaption of omegaverse to be introduced to mainstream media (per chapter on Yaoi and Slash). The most advantageous rendition of this genre would include a heterosexual main pairing with a male homosexual secondary pairing in an action or fast-paced science fiction or dystopia setting. Other additional resonance could be built in with social commentary, especially that pertaining to the influence of government on citizen's personal lives.

2016-2017- This time will serve as a window of opportunity for Japanese singers to make their way into US American markets. This opportunity is entirely contingent on securing a place in the cast of a film rendition of George Takei's musical autobiography. Such a casting would prove to be a foothold into the popular consciousness of Americans and could springboard Japanese artists into major market success.

2022-2027- Second window of opportunity for an omegaverse narrative or franchise to become popular in the USA.

2025- Best time for a South Korean film or animation to hit mainstream American media. Targeting the Hacker Gen as they enter their post-collegiate slump, the primary transnational resonance would be the struggle of 20-somethings adapting to a world more imperfect and disillusioning than expected. While Korea currently holds the largest per capita share of 20-somethings, the narrative would need to be cultivated *now* while, metaphorically, that oven is still hot, or in plainer speech, while all the pressures are still in place to create a plurality of stories resonating on this topic, for one to encompass enough resonance points (e.g. intergenerational strife, evolving gender roles and norms, skin hunger, professional precocity) to propel it to the head of the trend of stories. Eleven years offers enough time for the story to circulate and establish firm roots, to be re-made or readapted to meet the needs of the American audience in the 2020s.

Addendum: Table of Contents Omake

An Omake is a parodic synopsis or scene that follows a chapter in a mange or an episode in an anime.

Addendum: Author's Note

"You are never really satisfied with your first book." This is the advice I give myself daily. It was told to me by a novelist colleague who is now a US Today bestselling author. I keep similar quotes as a litany in my head as I work through the second edition of this book. (There may yet need to be a third edition, but I hope not.) On good days, I think of Ira Glass's advice[1] to beginners of creative work. On days when I'm coming out of the darkness of much of this material, I think of George Orwell's quote:

> Writing a book is a horrible, exhausting struggle, like a long bout with some painful illness. One would never undertake such a thing if one were not driven on by some demon whom one can neither resist nor understand.

This book is, at best, a journalistic expose on our culture, and at worst, a work of creative nonfiction ruminating on my experiences at anime conventions on the East Coast and at home. I'm at the point now, where many authors find themselves, where the book has to be done, but it may never be as finished as I would like it to be.

I hope it stimulates intellectual conversations at anime cons. I hope it lends some legitimacy to new and growing art form of fanfiction and of the new ways people are connecting to one another and effecting one

---

[1] https://www.youtube.com/watch?v=PbC4gqZGPSY

another. I hope it gives the vocabulary to individuals who are passionate about being an Otaku, but don't know how to describe how they feel or what they experience.

Since much of my goals in creating this work orbit around the idea of education, all of the profits I garner from the sale of this book will be put toward the alleviation of my student debt. When my education is paid off, and if this book is still turning a profit at that point, half of the proceeds will go to a non-profit organization with a mission to promote internationalism and understanding of Asian culture. The remainder will be used for my continuing education or my education of others.

In a few final words, thank you, reader, for spending your time with this book. In the words I often give in closing my emails.

I hope this helps.

Sincerely,
M. "Anego" Jean

PS- A soundtrack for this book can be found here: http://8tracks.com/softpowerpunch-428/soundtrack-for-snapshots-japanophilia-and-otaku

Addendum: Discard Pile

This addendum is for ideas that were not developed into chapters but are worth scribing.

God's Gonna Trouble the Water
- Drawing parallels from the victims/experiences/repercussions of Hurricane Katrina (and Rita) in the USA (2005) and the 2011 Tsunami in Japan
- Healing through Art for victims of public trauma
- The Wolf Children film's usage of the power of water
- Children and mass trauma
- Yeat's Stolen Child – "For the world's more full of weeping than you can understand" "the solemn eye'd"
- The Lost Post Office (in X prefecture) where victims can mail postcards to lost friends and families from the disaster and the New Orleans Kid Camera Project which allowed children to create films about their experiences in post-Katrina NOLA
- Private trauma vs (mass) public trauma
- Photogenic pain and loss: property loss, loss of lives, livelihood, and innocence

Is Japanese Culture "Cool"?
It depends on whom you ask. Some American teenagers, who watch anime or spend much of their time

immersed in JRPGs, Japan is the ultimate pinnacle of coolness. When these children grow up, they may look on Japanese culture with a sense of nostalgia and fondness. Still other American adults will perceive Japanese culture as the media has portrayed it to be: a source of both sophistication and wackiness, the land of both ancient tea ceremonies and selfie sticks.

This begs the question: art sphere will be aware of this visual trend in media. "Cuteness" has invaded our styles in both simplistic pop art (Thank you, Hello Kitty) and darker motifs as artists turn the idea of innocence on its head. For those outside of art discipline, however, cute things from Japan are not immediately recognizable as Japanese. A person on the street would think of several descriptors of Hello Kitty, such as "pink", "cute", or "for children", before coming up with association of "Japanese". Unbeknownst to the American pedestrian is that much of Hello Kitty's success is due to licensing to American companies, which have in turn adapted their products to American needs and desires. This may also be the source of the separation of the brand from Japanese culture.

Personally, I'd say it is "classy" and sometimes "cute" but not particularly "cool".

Why are Japan and the USA both preoccupied with "epicness"?

In Japan, it has to do with the legacy of losing WWII. They face the knowledge that a super power conquered them and to conquer it in turn requires an epic effort.

In the USA, it has to deal with the failure of the American Dream. We are told when we are children that we can do anything we put our minds to, and that rich men come from hard working entrepreneurs. This is untrue, and we struggle with reconciling the America we are taught about as schoolchildren and the America we live in as adults. This mental debate is channeled into our play and fantasies—we imagine that we can be that hero that conquers unimaginable odds, since in our real lives we do have those undefeatable foes, and have no superpower to help us secure success.

Genderbending and Gender Swapping

These two term refer to a phenomenon in fan fiction wherein a character's gender is changed, usually from male to female. Sometimes the character's name is changed as well. This is to allow female writers to closer identify with male protagonists and to make those characters deal with the author's own gender issues. It also offers an alternative to the m-preg and omegaverse way of solving this issue.

There has been MUCH writing about gender-bending and gender-swapping in academia, and so I decided to leave that line of reasoning out of my

Does the culture of anime cons differ regionally?

Yes. Anime cons are effected by the local culture where they are located. Cons are staffed by locals, so their culture will impact the culture of their work and their values on the con. Also, resources impact the offerings of a con. For example: Cons in the Boston area often have MIT professors give panels, making those cons to have strong academic content and thus a huge draw for con-goers who travel to cons is the intellectual conversation had there. In the mid-Atlantic area, where the culture is a blend of New England efficiency and Southern Hospitality, community places a large part in the draw and "feel" of the cons. (Pennsylvanian Quaker influence also attributes to this.)

On a larger scale, East Coast cons focus more on the Otaku community, markets (i.e. dealers' room and artist alley,) and performances while West Coast cons focus more on Cosplay (especially in California where haute couture is more accessible to a population that is more affluent) and Gaming (Silicon Valley influence).

There's also something to be said for the fact that there is a much larger Japanese-American population on the West Coast versus the East Coast. This too, changes the feel and expectations of anime cons.

What is the feasibility of an Ameri-con overseas?

Japan has gained great amounts of soft power thanks to anime cons in the USA. Is it feasible for the US to improve its international public image by hosting Ameri-cons overseas, modeled after the cons for Japanese culture promotion here in the US?

Not right now. America's melting pot culture, plurality of identities within its nation-state, and high amount of screen time and social time spent on the internet predisposes it for con culture and con success. Foreign countries' populaces would need to have a larger proportion of their self-identities formed in online communities and post-geographic cultures in order for such cons to be a success. They are certainly on their way, as we see cons popping up in Western Europe. It may be more likely to be successful in five years, or so, with the right type of franchises backing the convention (Marvel, for sure, but also Disney and, maybe in ten years, American video game firms).

Why do anime characters have big eyes?

The main players of early Japanese anime in the 1950s and 1960s were big fans of contemporary Disney animation styles. Disney characters had big eyes, so their characters had big eyes. The eye-shape evolved over time to what it is today.

Why do we like Anime?

Some people simply like the Japanese aesthetic, much like how many overseas liked Disney films for their catchy tunes and bright colors, many Americans like the animation style, deep textures, and a smaller sense of space (smaller spaces make scenes seem more familiar for urban Americans, while American media often is set in grander, more wide open spaces for the large proportion of America living in suburban and rural areas). For others, the primary appeal is the content. In the 1990s, that was stories targeting an audience overlooked by domestic television media. Nowadays, its stories that integrate or focus on the influence of technology on our lives, as well as darker stories for our darker times. Japanese artists and audiences do not flinch from using tragedy, and so there is a cathartic appeal in these narratives from Japan when US Americans are struggling and do not wish to be placated by a Disney happy ending.

Scraps

- I don't ever say "art informs society", but perhaps I should.
- Takarazuka
- "She turned me into a NEET!"
  -"A neet?!"
  "…I got better."
- (Sexual) consent as a metaphor for possessing power over another. Especially as rape culture intensifies.
- Muteness as a common trope in fan fiction. Especially for disenfranchised or disaffected populations that feel voice-less for some reason.
- For first time a generation of Americans had access to artifacts and influence of a subculture which was unfettered by geographic distribution. They could acquire artifacts and eventually would exhibit hallmarks of this new culture. In suburban areas, this new culture was exemplified as buying Japanese culture turned into producing a culture of fanworks: websites, artwork, stories reflecting activation of the primary Japanese culture and the secondary Otaku culture they assimilated within their psyches. Mores, values, aesthetics, language all influenced by this third culture. In urban settings, development of anime conventions more highly visible, reflecting a departure from the norm as these events included

markets, education, and community building institution (cultural edifices).

- The Otaku phenomenon is intriguing to study but also an essential middle step when tracing the evolution of fan communities in the USA as a 1st generation cultural phenomenon free from geographic confines with concrete ties to internationalism and globalization. These ties make it a salient edifice of the fan community and growing fannish culture.

Addendum: "A Feminist Walks into Gamergate and Walks Out on the Side of the MRAs" a teaser for <u>Snapshots of American Culture: The Gamers</u>

This book is to be released December 2016.

August 2014 saw a precipitous rise in the public awareness of the deep seated sexism and misogyny within videogame culture. Two events highlighted the chauvinism. First a climax in the hate campaign against videogame designer Zoe Quinn, who was the target of slanderous remarks that her games received good reviews on the site Kotaku from sleeping with the critics. When an actor, most well-known for his role in the Geek classic Firefly, echoed the virulent opinion of these malcontents, he coined the #Gamergate tag, and become a spearhead and point of legitimization for the anti-women movement.

A few days after this debacle, Anita Sarkeesian, an infamous videogame culture critic most well-known for her "Tropes Vs. Women in Videogames" webseries, cancelled her upcoming keynote address at Utah State University after receiving a threat of a mass-shooting at the venue, and the school not taking necessary steps to ensure her, and her audience's, security.

The videogame community is polarized: on one hand, you have feminists (or feminist allies) who believe that much of videogame culture is misogynistic and wish for this to change by increasing the visibility of games that have more even-handed portrayals of gender. One the other hand, are a select few, but very powerful and well organized, male gamers who believe that women are taking over their art form and calling for the censorship of their favorite games. It is important to note that the goals of one side do not respond or address the goals of the other. In plainer terms, the goals of the sides are not mutually exclusive, as one would believe them to be, considering the fiery opposition and tension between them.

I consider myself in the first camp, but, in an exercise of empathy, let me try to address the calls to action of the male minority. In reverse order, they believe with absolute certainty that women are calling for the censorship of their favorite games. I have no idea from where this idea originated. No artist nor journalist would ever call for or endorse censorship. It is contrary to their self-interest to promote state-mandating of art and eliminating free speech. The notion is groundless and only exists to give a fervent fire and invoke the idea of rights being infringed.

This leads us to the first call of action against women who are supposedly taking over the videogame art form, threatening men's historical and traditional center place in this culture. **These men are grievously upset by the idea of women-creators in their art.**

This is the crux of their argument, and the point from which all the hate starts. **Why are they experiencing this emotional response?**

Bear with me for a contextual tangent. I studied political science in uni, and during my sophomore year, I studied the United Nation's Declaration of Human Rights. This document was created on the heels of the Second World War, and was adopted by the UN in 1948. Article 27 in this historical document details a universal right to art. At the time of learning that the UN included such a right in the same document that mandated a freedom from slavery and torture, I was mystified. I agree that art is important, but is it truly THAT important?

Yes, it is. Art is a type of expression that all individuals utilize. We communicate through our paintings, our songs, and dance. While some artists live and die for their art, no person is untouched by some form of art. It permeates our culture and our lives. On the level of the individual, certain people are inclined towards certain arts: one who has aptitude to visualize three dimensional space may become a successful architect, one who has high color distinction and love of textures may enjoy fashion design, a lover of words may write, and so on.

In the USA, while each person has a right to art and to create, we do not protect all artists equally. While it is easy to see the community split apart on the lines of race and class, we must not forget that gender also plays its part in shaping of the art community. Men are regularly excluded from the USian art community. How? Simply put, making art, in nine cases out of ten, is seen as an anti-masculine activity. Men who are artists are not

as masculine as their non-creative peers, especially in
blue collar culture. This idea is wrapped up with the
common preconceived notion that artists, especially
those in visual arts, are effeminate or gay. Want to be
fashion designer? Painter? Composer? God forbid,
dancer? It is hard to partake in any of these forms
without your masculinity being called into question by
both women and men.

Now, of course, not all art forms in the US are
subject to this split, however, the rift does cause pressure
on the forms where men are in charge, and in these
forms we see a sort of hypermasculinity emerge. In
literature. In rap music. And now, in videogames.

A blue-collar man cannot say he is fond of
drawing, but he can say he designs characters for
videogames. A boy in the projects cannot say he enjoys
composing classical music, but he can say he creates
music for FPS games. A teenaged young man cannot say
he storytelling or thinking of different ways to tell a
story, but he can be an RPG script writer.

As women start invading these roles, these men
are, rightfully so, afraid of the idea that their outlet for
art will no longer be seen as a masculine occupation of
their time and a manly way to utilize their talents. I don't
think that these thoughts are ever expressed in such
words, but the undercurrent is there.

These men have a basic human right to art. We
have create a society that alienates them from that right,

and so they have clung to the few art forms that we allow them to be a part of and maintain their integrity.

In conclusion, I am in complete support of men being allowed to participate in and create art without their integrity and manliness being called into question. We, as feminists, need to support men in their right to art as much as we support women, and as broadly. If we eliminate the dire need for a male haven of art, we will alleviate the reflex, gut-reaction of right infringement, disenfranchisement, and disempowerment.

www.ingramcontent.com/pod-product-compliance
Lightning Source LLC
Chambersburg PA
CBHW071405280526
45787CB00001B/443